T0275353

JAPAN

AN ILLUSTRATED HISTORY

ILLUSTRATED HISTORIES FROM HIPPOCRENE

The Arab World
Arizona
The Celtic World
China
Cracow
Egypt
England
France
Greece
India
Ireland
Israel
Italy
Korea
London
Mexico
Moscow
Paris
Poland
Poland in World War II
Romania
Russia
Sicily
Spain
Tikal
Vietnam
Wales

JAPAN
AN ILLUSTRATED HISTORY

SHELTON WOODS

HIPPOCRENE BOOKS, INC.
New York

For information, address:
Hippocrene Books, Inc.
171 Madison Avenue
New York, NY 10016

Book design and composition by Susan A. Ahlquist.

ISBN 0-7818-0989-4

Cataloging-in-Publication data available from the Library of Congress.

Printed in the United States of America.

For my sisters, Michelle and Rachel.

Acknowledgments

This book was made possible by many people directly and indirectly involved in the project. I'm grateful to Jerome and Kazuko Klena for their help in obtaining photos and illustrations for this book. Jerry was also very helpful in reading and commenting on the manuscript. My thanks also go to the following organizations and individuals who allowed me to use illustrations for this book: Shinjuku Historical Museum, Tokyo National Museum, Aizu Museum of Waseda University, Chiba Prefectural Sekiyado-jo Museum (Hiroshi Shimada, Senior Researcher), The Koga City Museum of History (Toshihiko Nagayo, Museum Curator), Jingu Chokokan Museum, Koudai Zenji Temple (Mr. Mamiya), and Shingoji Temple (Mr. Taniuchi, Chief Priest). Anne Kemper at Hippocrene Books was encouraging and helpful throughout the entire process of writing this book.

While they were not directly involved with the project, it certainly would not have been completed without encouragement from Brad Chaney, Dirk Carlson, Milt Umphrey, Bill

Atkinson, Scott Schaeffer, and all those at Valley West. Karen Kelsch and Valencia Garrett in the dean's office were also of immeasurable help during the writing of this book. Peter Buhler, Todd Shallat, and Mike Blankenship always provide their unreserved support for my writing and research projects.

My son Lindsay taught me fly-fishing during the writing of this book. It was a great opportunity to reflect on the past, and to anticipate a future of fishing streams, rivers, and lakes with him. Karen, my wife, is my severest (and most trusted) critic, and most loyal friend. Thank you for your help on this book, which was only an extension of your love and support that I feel every day.

Table of Contents

Table of Contents

Introduction

After the machine guns ceased their deadly fire, and after the last body was pulled from the muck of trench warfare, the victors of World War I gathered at the French town of Versailles to fashion a treaty that all the winners could accept. Participants at the Versailles parley carried with them a range of expectations: France wanted to make sure Germany would pay for its aggression; Woodrow Wilson, America's twenty-eighth president, hoped that his proposal for a council of nations would take form; and China hoped that it would reacquire foreign-held Chinese territory. For all the pomp and ceremony at Versailles, however, one of the most amazing aspects of the meeting was Japan's designation as one of the five "great powers." Joining Japan in this elite group were the United States, Britain, France, and Italy. Japan's status as a "great power" in 1919 was astounding not only because it was the only Asian nation to hold that title, but also because it demonstrated Japan's meteoric rise as a lead player on the international stage. Only half a century earlier, the West had considered Japan a backward, unindustrialized, feudal, economically irrelevant state. Yet, between 1868 and 1918, Japan experienced remarkable economic, social, and military transformations. During that fifty-year period Japan had industrialized, acquired an empire, and militarily defeated the imperial nations of Russia and China. Japan was not content with these achievements. During the 1930s and 1940s it created the unparalleled Greater East Asian Co-Prosperity Empire. Following World War II, it became the planet's leading banking institution and an economic superpower. Before the end of the twentieth century, Japan solidified itself in the pantheon of history's world powers.

Reading through the pages of human history, it is difficult to find a more unlikely story than the one found in the following pages. Japan had Asia's strongest military and economy in the twentieth century, and was the first industrialized nation outside of the West. Its prominence in these spheres is astounding given the fact that Japan is a cluster of a few islands in the Pacific Ocean. Japan's historic imperial capital, Kyoto, is more than five hundred miles from the Asian Continent. Thus, we cannot compare Japan's geographical isolation with that of England, which sits only twenty-one miles from continental Europe.

Japan's total land area is roughly equal to that of the U.S. State of Montana. Of Japan's limited land space, only 20 percent is arable. Most of Japan's topography is mountainous, which makes for beautiful landscape views, but hinders farming efforts to feed a large population. And Japan has many people on its shores. As far back as 1600, Japan's populace was more numerous than that of any European state. One hundred years later, Japan was the most urbanized country on the planet, and Edo, the shogun's capital, the world's largest city. At the turn of the twenty-first century, Japan continues to rank among the world's top ten most populous nations.

With limited space and a large population, one might imagine that Japan's basis for its superpower status must be its extensive natural resources. In truth, Japan lacks significant natural resources. It was Japan's lack of such treasures that spared it from the encroaching Western imperialists of the nineteenth century. Today Japan remains the world's largest importer of oil, cotton, timber, and scores of other such materials.

The puzzle of Japan's greatness grows even more complicated when one considers its historical isolation. Since the seventh century A.D., there has been no significant immigration into Japan. It remains a very homogenous population. As shown later in this history, Japan adopted a policy in the seventeenth century wherein it was against the law for anyone to depart from or arrive on Japanese soil without permission from the shogun's advisors. Very few ever asked for such permission, and even fewer were granted sanction to leave or visit the sacred islands. This statute remained in place for more than two hundred years. For two centuries Japan spun a web around itself and settled into a self-manufactured social cocoon.

An ethnically homogenous population with limited outside interference has its advantages. When there is no immigration, it is easier to generate a sense of unity, nationalism, and an "us" versus "them" attitude. At the same time, isolation has its dangers. It breeds paranoia. The same elements that create national pride can deteriorate into a disdain for anyone who is different.

Our journey into Japan's past begins by examining the seeds planted thousands of years ago that sprouted into the world's most improbable superpower. Japan's foundational worldview was largely shaped by its geographical location on our planet.

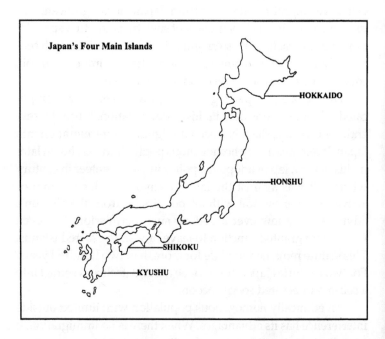

Japan's Four Main Islands

HOKKAIDO

HONSHU

SHIKOKU

KYUSHU

The Shaping of Japan's World
(4000 B.C.–A.D. 250)

Geography

There was a time when Japan's main islands were geographically joined to the Asian mainland. We know this because there are ancient skeletal remains of large animals in Japan. These animals, including elephants and rhinoceroses, did not arrive in Japan by swimming across the hundreds of miles that now separate Japan's islands from the Asian continent. Archaeologists claim that these large mammals walked across contiguous land bridges thousands of years ago. Evidence of these journeys is found throughout Japan.

The four main islands of Japan are Kyushu, Honshu, Shikoku, and Hokkaido. Japan's historic economic, political, and social centers are found on Honshu and Kyushu. The northernmost island of Hokkaido was generally ignored by the Japanese until the nineteenth century.

While some nations are culturally divided by north/south boundaries, it is best to understand the differences in Japan according to east/west regions. Japan's bloody sixteenth-century civil war was based on east/west military alliances. Domestic rivalries date to the first inhabitants who entered Japan. More than six thousand years ago, migrating groups from Siberia in the north and Korea in the south populated portions of Japan. In northwestern Japan, Caucasoid peoples entered Japan via land bridges or simple sailing ships. They survived by gathering nuts and berries, hunting wild game, and fishing. As they moved south, they were met by a stronger set of peoples who were of Mongoloid stock. Japan's first western inhabitants were migrants from Korea and, perhaps, portions of China. Since districts of Kyushu are only a hundred miles from the Korean Peninsula, it is likely that Korean individuals, families, and clans moved east to an area that promised greater security. The island of Tsushima, between Korea and Japan, was also a convenient staging ground where boat people rested as they made the trek from the peninsula to western Japan.

While the Mongoloid peoples conquered the weaker Caucasoid inhabitants, also known as Ainu, there was some integration of these groups. This explains the varied facial features among Japanese. While most Mongoloid men do not have facial hair, it is common to see Japanese men with full beards. This variety among the Japanese points to the early interaction between the Ainu and Mongoloid inhabitants.

From the earliest days of Japanese civilization, there has been contact between Korea and Japan. This illustration from 1763 depicts Korean envoys making their way to Edo (Tokyo).

This is a nineteenth-century coat from the Hokkaido-dwelling Ainu people.

Jimmu and Creation Myths of Japan

During the eighth century A.D. the Japanese aristocrats, taking their cue from the Chinese, recorded Japan's past. In 712 the *Kojiki* was written, which was a history of the Japanese state. Eight years later a second national history was published entitled *Nihon Shoki*. These volumes included stories of Japan's origin. These legends were orally transmitted until they were placed in writing.

The story begins before there was a heaven or earth. Chaos and void governed an undefined universe. From this emptiness something like vapor arose and heaven was created. In heaven three deities emerged and they are called the Three Creating Deities. Meanwhile, just as heaven emerged from a formless void, so too did the planets and galaxies. After millions of years, earth produced thousands of gods that inhabited the world. The earth remained in chaos and so heaven's Three Creating Deities chose to send the divine couple, Izanagi and Izanami, to earth. These two gods created other gods and the islands of Japan.

Izanami died while giving birth to the god of fire and her body was taken to the underworld. Izanagi traveled to the world of the dead to see his mate. When he arrived, Izanagi caught a glimpse of his lover's decomposing body. Offended by the foul sight, Izanagi fled the underworld and bathed to remove the pollution that he incurred. As he bathed, he gave birth to Amaterasu from his left eye, Tsukiyomi from his right eye, and Susa-no-o from his nose. Some believe that these three offspring correspond to the three cosmic realms of heaven, earth, and humanity. Amaterasu, the sun goddess, was assigned to the heavens, with Tsukiyomi, the moon deity, as her assistant. In the course of time, Susa-no-o, the storm god, visited his sister, Amaterasu. After consuming too much alcohol, Susa-no-o destroyed rice farms and fences that protect rice paddies. He intruded on Amaterasu, as she was in her weaving room, and threw excrement into the hall. This caused Amaterasu to run in fear and hide, thus depriving the world of light. Many gods tried to cajole Amaterasu out of hiding. They offered her jewels, a lewd dance was performed for her, and a mirror was made so that she could see her beauty. When she emerged to take the jewels and mirror, the gods strategically placed ropes to keep Amaterasu from returning to the cave. They also believed that Susa-no-o needed to be punished for his earlier behavior. They cut his hair and pulled out his beard, fingernails, and toenails. One of his acts of penance was to return to his sister and present her with a sword.

Amaterasu gave birth and one of her descendents, Ninigi, was sent to Japan to provide rule and guidance. He was given Amaterasu's sword, mirror, and jewels in order to attest to her blessing and his authority. Ninigi ruled western Japan with this authority and in the course of time one of his offspring, Jimmu, asserted that it was the duty of Amaterasu's descendents to rule all under heaven under one roof. Taking the three pieces of the imperial regalia (mirror, jewels, sword), Jimmu marched on the eastern clans. When victory was not forthcoming, Jimmu deduced that the problem was that his army was attacking with Amaterasu (the sun) directly in front of it. The generals agreed that the more appropriate approach was from the east so that the sun would be behind their backs. Jimmu and his troops reached their new home base, the Yamato Plain, by using the Inland Sea. From this base of operations, they conquered clans that would not submit to his rule. Finally, on the first day of the lunar calendar year 660 B.C. (February 11), Jimmu ascended to the throne and began his reign as Japan's first emperor—an imperial line that continues to this day.

The existence of Emperor Jimmu is not verified in history. The first emperor from the Yamato line that can be historically verified, and even this is quite unclear, is the tenth emperor, Sujin. There is more information about the reign of Sujin in the *Kojiki* than that of any of the earlier emperors, save for Jimmu. In the Japanese historical chronicles, Ōjin (A.D. 346–395) is said to be the fifteenth of the Yamato emperors. It is possible that he, in fact, was the founder of the Yamato dynasty.

Jōmon Japan (2500–250 B.C.)

The earliest societies in Japan existed during what is known as Jōmon Japan. The term Jōmon is taken from the type of pottery associated with this culture. Using various ropes that were pressed into the clay, leaving a permanent pattern on the vessels or bowls, Jōmon peoples elaborately decorated their pottery. The limited information we have about Jōmon times is solely based on archaeological evidence. Yet, even from this one source we can glean some insight into what life was like in Japan's early societies.

Jōmon pottery is characterized by decorations from rope imprints.

Artifacts from Jōmon times include vases, axe tools, and arrowheads.

Jōmon peoples were not farmers. Reliance on hunting wild game and gathering edible material from forests for sustenance made life precarious at best. Various skeletons from this era demonstrate that malnutrition stunted the development of the Jōmon adolescents. Most skeletal remains from this time indicate that wisdom teeth were barely used, which leads archaeologists to assert that the lifespan during this era was approximately thirty years.

Archaeological evidence indicates certain religious aspects to Jōmon civilization. Special caskets were created for the dead, while some of the deceased's bones were painted red. Such rituals for the dead prove that there was a belief that life continued beyond the grave. Moreover, like most early civilizations, the most important gods of the Jōmon times were related to fertility. Phallic-shaped stones and statues representing women with large breasts, bloated stomachs, and oversized hips appear to be the items that the people used to summon metaphysical help. Jōmon peoples must have reached out for transcendent help, especially as the amount of wild game decreased and foraging for food became more difficult.

One final aspect of this civilization was its abrupt end. It is possible that an increased population with the concomitant decrease in food supply led to a severe famine that devastated Jōmon society. More likely, however, it was the emergence of a more sophisticated society that proved the undoing of Jōmon people. This society introduced two important elements to Japan that the indigenous residents could not compete with: the economic stability of an agrarian community, and the use of metal for weapons and tools.

Yayoi Japan (250 B.C.–A.D. 250)

About three centuries before Christ, Jōmon society was displaced by a more advanced civilization. This new cultural group is now referred to as Yayoi, the term coming from a location name on the periphery of Tokyo where, in 1948, a discovery was made that confirmed the presence of a post-Jōmon, pre-Yamato society. Many changes distinguish Yayoi as a time in which greater sophistication in culture and the economy marked a new civilization on the islands. Such dramatic changes occurred only one other time in Japan, and that was during the Meiji Era (1868–1912) when Japan moved into an industrialized/modern state.

It is probable that the knowledge of rice farming and the use of metals came to western Japan from Korea. The importance of rice in Asian history in general, and Japan in particular, cannot be overestimated. Rice is what made Japan a prosperous nation; it united communities, sustained Japan's large population, was the basis of taxation, created an aristocratic hierarchy, and was the primary monetary entity used throughout Japan.

Yayoi society was centered on rice cultivation. This agricultural endeavor required a group effort because it was extremely labor intensive. Growing rice demanded that the land be shaped into flat paddies that could be flooded and drained. It was imperative that the water level in the paddy remain at a particular height during the planting, growing, and harvesting periods. Yayoi farmers planted the rice one stalk at a time and harvested it in the same manner. Following the

Pottery from the Yayoi period.

harvest, the crop had to be dried, and then the seed separated from the husk. With such an undertaking, we understand why the earliest villages and clans developed around the rice fields. Economically, this grain was important because it could be stored. Therefore, food was available during the winter and typhoon seasons when it was impossible to fish or cultivate the ground. Increased prosperity due to rice-agriculture gave rise to other economic endeavors, including animal husbandry and trade with neighboring states.

Yayoi communities slowly moved east. They brought with them the knowledge of rice cultivation and simple irrigation, reaching modern-day Tokyo by 200 A.D. Based on archaeological evidence, it is posited that Yayoi Japan supported a population of over 600,000 people.

In A.D. 57, communities in Japan had sufficient political and economic sophistication to send envoys to China's Han court. The rise and fall of Yayoi Japan chronologically matches that of China's Han dynasty (202 B.C.–A.D. 221). Records indicate that some type of diplomatic relations took place between Yayoi communities and Han China. By the third century A.D., Chinese records show that there were one hundred countries in Japan, ranging from one thousand to seventy thousand households in each one. At least thirty of these communities had direct relations with China's post-Han kingdom of Wei (A.D. 221–265). Japan's countries, as described in early Chinese records, included the emerging clan communities. These kinship-based communities are known as *uji*, or clans, and are marked by four characteristics.

During Yayoi Japan, the *uji* communities created definite geographical boundaries for their territories. While it is too early to designate these areas as states or even provinces, they are called countries by the Chinese, which we might interpret as self-contained societies that were politically autonomous, apart from recognizing the power in distant China. Thus the first distinctive characteristic of early *uji* groups was that they marked their geographical boundaries to demonstrate that specific land belonged to the community. We also learn from Chinese and Japanese records, as well as archaeological findings, that shamans and priestesses were the leaders of the various *uji*. Their duty was to communicate with ancestors and the inanimate spirits that surrounded the world of the living. There is evidence that females dominated this second aspect of Yayoi culture. In the third century A.D., the Chinese record keepers noted that the only person who could bring order and lead the various *uji* was a priestess who was revered because of her "witchcraft."

Religion was the third aspect of *uji* communities that distinguished them from each other. The evolving nature of religion in Japan is noted further below, but as *uji* mapped out their geographical boundaries, each also adopted a god for the community. This deity became the patron for the village and was the exclusive god of the *uji*. There is no indication that one *uji* took up arms against another to claim its neighbor's god and this may be because many of the *uji* gods were represented by a physical feature in nature, whether a river, mountain, tree, etc., within the communities' geographical boundaries. The *uji's* god came to symbolize the founder of the particular clan. Thus, each *uji* had its own leader, physical border, and god. The final characteristic among *uji* families was that each village had its own shrine where the clan's deity was revered. While this worship was relatively simple, it does provide a lens through which we can see the maturation of Japan's earliest metaphysical beliefs.

The Way of the Gods—Shinto Thought

Though there is little information about Japan's earliest societies, we do know that religion was of paramount importance to the first people that lived on Japanese soil. The first written Chinese documentation we have about the Japanese was recorded in the third century A.D. and it includes a section that details their preoccupation with metaphysical matters. The *Kojiki* and *Nihon Shoki* lay out the history of Japan in terms of a land that the gods shaped and chose to bless with their presence. Jōmon people carved gods of fertility from rock and sought spiritual guidance through their reverence of these statues. During Yayoi times, bronze and iron were developed in Japan. Iron was used for weapons and agricultural tools, but bronze was used for making bells. These bells were not used outside of religious ceremonies. Reportedly, tapping a bell awakened the gods when individuals prepared to worship the deities.

Shinto became the state religion of Japan. This religion, in contrast to Islam, Christianity, and Buddhism, does not have a founder, and its evolving nature matches its somewhat abstract notions of good, evil, and human responsibility. While Buddhism asserts that selfishness is the source of suffering, and other religions have a divinely appointed set of moral codes, early Shinto tradition did not concern itself with such things. In short, the idea of good and bad, at least in the realm of early Shinto thought, was absent. Shinto ascribed calamity and sorrow in this world to the problem of pollution. The source of pollution was with the gods. As noted earlier, Izanagi became contaminated when he viewed his mate's decomposing body and was constrained to purify himself through bathing. Furthermore, Susa-no-o spread pollution by his vile acts in Amaterasu's presence. As pollution destroyed the harmony in heaven, it also produced chaos on earth. Eventually the Japanese categorized pollution or *tsumi* as malevolent acts committed in heaven and on earth. *Tsumi* in human beings is brought on by touching a corpse, contact with blood, desecrating rice paddies belonging to a shrine, and illness. If one is polluted, it is imperative to become purified. This is done by bathing, preferably in very warm water.

At a community level, there are very few rites to keep an entire village pure. One that is noteworthy, however, is the Ōharae (the Great Purification Ceremony). This rite is related to the gods' expulsion of Susa-no-o after his vile acts against his sister, Amaterasu. Villagers gather and take a doll that has symbolically absorbed all the offenses of the community. The doll is then tossed into a river to be swept away by the water, hopefully all the way to the sea. The doll takes with it all the pollution that was present in the village. There are striking similarities between this ritual and the ancient Hebrew ceremony of the scapegoat.

Another theme in Japan's religion is the identification of gods, or *kami*. In fact, Shinto means the "way of the *kami*." The

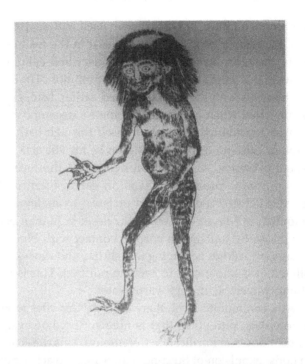

Much of early Japanese religion has animistic overtones. Thus, there are many supposed malevolent spirits that the Japanese feared. This is an artist's rendering of the "Kappa," a river imp who is both good and bad (sometimes helping humans, other times drowning people). This imp needs to keep the top of his head filled with water.

This is a male Shinto deity from the eleventh century.

greatest of the gods, such as Amaterasu, are identified in Japan's oral and written traditions. There are, however, thousands of minor or lesser gods in the pantheon of Shintoism. These gods are identified as an object that inspires awe or a notion of transcendence, such as a mountain, a river, a waterfall, a tree, or other natural wonder. As the *uji* developed during Yayoi times, each clan chose a god that it would worship. This god became identified as the clan's first father or mother.

Simplicity typifies both the shrine architecture and the nature of Shinto worship. Most shrines are characterized by a simple shelter. A typical act of worship is to stand in front of the shrine, clap your hands once (to get the attention of the god), and utter a brief prayer. Some adherents to this faith might scatter small portions of salt or rice near the shrine as an act of purification.

While Shinto worship remained simple, its connection with the history of Japan created a faith that became the foundation for an imperial rule. As one dominant clan emerged on the Yamato Plain and subdued its surrounding rivals, it chose the mightiest god, the sun goddess, as its patron deity. Legends about imperial rule of Japan centered on a descendent of Amaterasu, the aforementioned Jimmu. This first emperor reportedly settled in the Yamato Plain and, with the imperial regalia of the mirror, jewels, and sword, ruled as a heavenly prince. Thus the emperor was equated with the greatest of all gods, and eventually came to be viewed as divine. The emperor's divinity was socially accepted in Japan until after World War II, when the West forced Emperor Hirohito to tell the Japanese nation that he was, in fact, mortal.

Shinto worship is uncomplicated though the architecture leading to a Shinto altar can be breathtaking. This is the entrance to the Shinto Shrine in Veno Park, Tokyo.

Transition from
Yayoi to Yamato Japan
(250–600)

It is during Yamato Japan (A.D. 250–600) that Japan's history becomes much clearer. Historians wish that the shift from Yayoi to Yamato were as lucid. What we do know about this transition is that a dominant power arrived on the Yamato Plain, particularly at the base of the sacred Mount Miwa. This force was unique from its rivals in that it had a cavalry. The Chinese chroniclers noted in their third-century description of Japan that horses had not yet been introduced. Thus horses were imported from China or Korea and were used to subjugate non-cooperative *uji*. Where did this force come from? There are at least three possibilities as to the origin of the Yamato power, and controversy surrounds each theory.

Japan's eighth-century chroniclers, and the subsequent avid nationalist historians, theorized that the Yamato rule was merely an extension of an imperial rule that began hundreds of years before Christ. The emperors' slow extension of suzerainty eventually engulfed all the renegade *uji*. One of the problems with this theory, apart from its flimsy evidence, is that there is a definite shift in society and social practices during the fourth century. For example, this period is marked by the construction of elaborate tombs for the leading powers. Known as the Kofun (or Tumulus) period (A.D. 250–500), evidence suggests that the leaders in this era were relatively new arrivals. There is also a sudden appearance of horses, which points to a change in the means of gaining and maintaining influence. Finally, Chinese observers noted that the dominant authority during the third century in Japan was a female shaman rather than a male emperor on the Yamato Plain.

During the twentieth century a Japanese scholar introduced a new theory regarding the ascendance of the Yamato *uji*. This second hypothesis is based upon events in China. During the third century, China's Han dynasty came to an end and a good number of tribes in northern China fled the ensuing chaos and migrated to the Korean Peninsula. The warriors in these tribes were effective horsemen and they used cavalry tactics to overpower their enemies. Since there is historical evidence that horses were not introduced into Japan until the third or fourth century, it is believed that these tribal warriors brought their horses with them in their quest to gain dominance in Japan. It is also of note that there was extensive interaction between Japan and Korea during the beginning of Yamato times. Something must have happened to increase the interaction between these two regions. For those who believe that an outside power established the Yamato line of rulers, it seems natural that these new rulers would keep close ties with their relatives on the mainland.

The final theory of the origin of the Yamato rulers centers on the aforementioned Ōjin. Noted as the fifteenth emperor of Japan, the legend surrounding his birth also has references to Korea. According to folklore, Ōjin's mother, obeying the orders she received in a trance, traveled to Korea and conquered portions of the peninsula. On her return, she gave birth to Ōjin, whom the gods made emperor because of his mother's obedience to the directions given to her in the trance.

The eighth-century histories of Japan have much to say about Ōjin, and one of ancient Japan's largest burial mounds is Ōjin's. It is located just southwest of the Yamato Plain in Izumi. The material found in this tomb and other such sites indicate that by the end of the fourth century, there was a shift in the duties and position of Japan's kings. Earlier rulers were primarily revered because of their abilities to conduct rites, rituals, and communication with the spirit world. By A.D. 400, however, and the enthronement of Ōjin, the king was politically powerful due to his military prowess. The tombs during this period are full of military instruments and material, which indicate an increased imperial interest in secular affairs. The dimension of Ōjin's tomb is 1,365 feet in length while his son's (Nintoku) burial mound is 1,580 feet long. These are considerably larger than the burial mounds of Japan's third- and fourth-century rulers. To build such tombs required a ruler to have thousands of workers at his or her disposal. Finally, the historical records suggest that a new succession of emperors began with Ōjin. Thus, though he is a fourth-century figure, it is possible that Ōjin moved into the Yamato area from Kyushu, or an area with strong ties to the Korean Peninsula, and established the beginning of an unbroken imperial line in Japan.

Whatever theory one accepts, it is clear that Japan's philosophical and political foundations were established during Yamato times. These ideologies include imperial rule, a strict social hierarchy, Confucianism, and Buddhism. These imported philosophies shaped Japan's worldview and we now turn our attention to these ethical ideals as they molded the Japanese.

Most children, at one time or another, play a game called "king of the hill." The object of the contest is to get to the highest point on a mound and keep all rivals off the peak. Often the hardest part of the game is not getting to the top; rather, it is staying there. In fact, the Chinese have a proverb that it is much easier to gain power than it is to keep it. How is it, then, that the Yamato clan maintained political and then imperial power for more than fifteen hundred years? The answer to this question is complex but it begins with rice.

The introduction of iron, new agricultural methods, and grains from the Asian continent increased food production in Japan. Families and clans grew in number and strength because of economic security. Yamato kings/emperors responded to the potentially destabilizing effects of more powerful families by ranking all the clans from the most powerful to the least. The two most powerful clans were directed to relocate to an area near the Yamato imperial court. These clans were designated the *omi* and *muraji*. Two incentives encouraged the top clans to move to the Yamato Plain. First, the emperor provided rice for these clans from the taxes that were brought in from the surrounding region. It was also promised that the future kings would take their brides from the *omi* and *muraji* daughters, thus making these outside clans the *gaiseki* (in-law) to the royal house. With the most powerful clans under the emperor's watchful eye, there was less likelihood that the strongest families would cause domestic problems. Furthermore, if there was a disturbance in the countryside, the emperor could call on the mightiest groups to squelch rural rebellions.

Japan's increased political and economic stability produced a society where there was time to learn from more sophisticated cultures. Korea was the closest landmass to Japan, and there is some evidence that Japan's presence on the Asian peninsula was so extensive that they had a colony, known as Mimana, on Korea's southeast tip. During the fifth and sixth centuries, China and Korea were politically unstable, though they remained culturally superior to Japan. There were members of the Japanese imperial court that wanted to integrate Chinese and Korean cultural elements into Japanese life. In particular, the Soga family, an influential clan in the Yamato court, was responsible for the spread of a foreign religion at the court. That religion was Buddhism.

Buddhism and Japan

Japan's indigenous religion was Shinto. As noted earlier, this faith was not adorned with complicated rituals or divine texts that explained human existence. Buddhism, on the other hand, was steeped in religious symbols, sophisticated ceremonies, elaborate artwork, and sacred writings. Buddhism originated in northern India about five centuries before Christ and slowly made its way east. By the time that it reached Korea, there were numerous elements of Chinese thought integrated into Buddhism. China was greatly revered by its border countries, and the fact that it had adopted Buddhism made the new religion even more appealing to other East Asian cultures.

According to tradition, Buddhism was offered to the Japanese in a *quid pro quo* agreement. A civil war on the Korean Peninsula constrained one of the competing states, Paekche, to appeal to Japan's court for aid. In return for this aid, the Paekche leader offered to introduce to the Japanese court a new faith that was sweeping through China. Japan sent military support to its Korean ally and in return, the Paekche leaders dispatched several Buddhist monks to introduce this new religion to Japan.

While there are various stories regarding Buddhism's entrance into Japan, it is clear that this foreign faith received a mixed reception at Japan's imperial court. The clans with deep roots in Japan did not want their indigenous Shinto beliefs to have any competition and so they opposed the introduction of Buddhism. On the other hand, the clans that were relatively recent transplants from Korea, namely the Soga clan, were eager to follow a religion from outside the area. A foreign faith would serve to legitimize the growing influence of the recently transplanted aristocratic families. The more recent immigrant families won the political battle against the entrenched clans. Japanese historians attribute the victory of Buddhism in Japan to a principal court advisor, Prince Shōtoku. A leader of the Soga clan, Shōtoku was appointed as a regent to the empress in 593. As a devout Buddhist, Shōtoku worked for the next thirty years to incorporate this faith into the imperial household. He

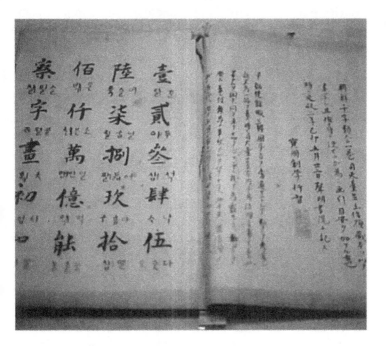

The Japanese language is a combination of Chinese and indigenous influence. This is a nineteenth-century dictionary of Korean.

is remembered for his introduction of numerous Chinese influences to Japan. It is possible that this one figure is given too much credit for the growth of Chinese influence in Japan, and that Shōtoku represents a movement as much as he does an individual.

The Seventeen-Article Constitution of 604

In 604 Shōtoku reportedly produced Japan's first enduring political document. Consisting of seventeen points, this essay is known as the Seventeen-Article Constitution. Its primary significance is that it demonstrated the court's desire to incorporate Chinese philosophy and religion into the Japanese political and social systems. Between the lines of this document we see the court's attempt to create an ethical system that was on par with the more sophisticated Chinese structure.

Shōtoku based the Seventeen-Article Constitution on Confucianism, Buddhism, and legalism. Because Japanese officials wanted their state to mature politically and socially, they feasted on a steady diet of continental ethical cuisine. The individual courses are explained in the following paragraphs.

Confucianism and Japan

The first line of the first article in Shōtoku's text is a direct quote from the Confucian *Analects*: "Harmony is to be cherished." It also ends with a Confucian notion that if harmony is maintained then "Everything can be accomplished." It is clear that this philosophy was to hold prominence in Japan. In fact, it governed Japanese ethics for the next thirteen centuries.

By the time Japan sought to borrow ideas from Confucianism, the philosophy's originator had been in the grave for a thousand years. Born into a world of political chaos, Confucius (551–479 B.C.) was the son of an insignificant noble. China was divided into numerous states—each hoping that it could achieve military superiority over its rivals. No one could bring unity to China. This did not stop Confucius from asserting that order and unity were possible. He boasted, "Were any prince to employ me, even in a single year a good deal could be done, and in three years everything could be accomplished." Confident that he could stop incessant warring throughout China, Confucius traveled from state to state seeking employment as an advisor to a prince or king. He believed that the answer to humanity's problem centered on virtue, relationships, and proper ritual.

Harmony between heaven and earth is a primary goal in Confucianism. This is achieved by the transformation of men (Confucius was chauvinistic in his teaching) from common brutes to gentlemen. He wanted men to cultivate virtue in their personal and public lives through the maintenance of proper relationships and the observance of prescribed rituals.

"To have friends coming from afar: is this not a delight." This first verse from the collected sayings of Confucius represents the major theme of relationships in Confucianism. According to Confucius, the problems in society and government are directly related to the breakdown of human relationships. Five human connections and the appropriate behavior for each one are carefully outlined in his teachings. The first of these is the bond between the emperor and his subjects. In this relationship, Confucius taught that heaven had placed the emperor on the throne, thus rebellion against the emperor was considered to be synonymous with fighting against heaven. Because of this teaching, the rulers of China, who were not democratically elected, received the support of the people because to do otherwise would mean that the people were falling away from virtue and the will of heaven.

The second union that must be properly nurtured is between father and son. An important term in Chinese philosophy is filial piety. This is the notion of the son's obligation to be obedient, subservient, and respectful to his father. The worst crime one could commit in China was for a son to slander or physically abuse his father. After a father's death, the son's responsibility to his father remained. The oldest male child was expected to set up an altar of remembrance for the deceased father. Confucianism asserts that by revering a deceased patriarch, the departed spirit finds comfort and his name is remembered among the living. One result of this teaching was that sons and eternal life became synonymous. According to proper ritual, only the son could carry on the father's name and conduct proper ancestor rites so that the soul would experience eternal peace.

The idea of eternal life and the priority given to father-son relations further damaged the perceived worth and dignity of Chinese women. Historically, it is difficult to find a civilization that treated women more poorly than the Chinese. Women were not considered human beings. If someone would knock at the door to see if anyone was home, and all the men were out of the house, the women would reply that no one was home. This was not because women did not want to invite guests in the house; it was because the women did not see themselves as people. Women were supposed to be obedient to three male figures in their lives: their fathers, husbands, and sons. Women were valued mainly because through birth they could produce male members of society.

The third relationship that Confucius spoke about was between husband and wife. Wives were to be completely subservient to their husbands. They were never to question their husbands nor show any sign of disrespect. A double standard existed in the sexual relationship between husband and wife. If it was discovered that a married woman was having an adulterous affair, the punishment was death. Meanwhile, men who could afford it usually had concubines or secondary wives. There was no penalty for this unfaithfulness.

A brother-to-brother relationship was also a subject that the *Analects* addressed. What is important in this affiliation is that the younger brother must obey the commands of his older brother. In most Asian societies there is a title of respect that is associated with an older brother, and younger siblings rarely call their older brother by his first name without placing a title of respect before it. This assures male hierarchy within the family structure.

Finally, Confucius taught that it was important for relationships between friends to be kept in order. The emphasis in this association was faithfulness. A true friend was one that would never betray a confidence and would remain loyal through good and bad times.

The chain that links virtue and relationships, according to Confucius, is proper ritual. Perhaps we can best understand this by using an example that we are more familiar with—the simple handshake. It is somewhat of a ritual that when we meet someone or say good-bye we shake hands. There are many potential emotions and unspoken feelings in a handshake. If someone is happy to see you, they can take your hand with both of theirs and give you a warm greeting, or, if they are mad at you, they can grab your hand and shake it fiercely. There is such a thing as a "dead fish" handshake when the hand you grasp seems limp and lifeless. Confucius might say that while there may be many ways that one goes about shaking a hand (or participating in a ritual) there is only one proper way for a handshake to be done. The details regarding ceremonies and rituals extended to the color and length of a coat one should wear on particular occasions.

During the days of Shōtoku, Confucian principles became the theme of the Japanese imperial court. Japan's many small states in this period were a symptom of political disunity. Confucianism offered the Japanese leaders a prescribed worldview where political and social unity would result in harmony.

Buddhism and the Seventeen-Article Constitution

Buddhism came to Japan through Korean channels. Though Japan enjoyed an indigenous metaphysical faith, the astounding

A tenth-century statue of the Eleven-Headed Kanon Bosatsu [the Compassionate Buddha].

growth of Buddhism's influence at the court is evidenced in the second article of Shōtoku's constitution: "With all your heart revere the three treasures. The three treasures are the Buddha, the *Dharma* (Buddhist Law) and the *Sangha* (the Buddhist monastic orders)." The reasons why the Japanese embraced this foreign faith are manifold. Many of the leading families were from Korea and China and so this religion strengthened their ties to their relatives on the Asian continent. Buddhism also offered Japan a worldview that dealt with the issues of life and death. While Confucianism focused on ethics, and Shinto explained the past, Buddhism sought to answer the nagging questions of why tragedy visits certain individuals, and what happens to a person after death.

By the time that Buddhism arrived in Japan it had undergone numerous changes from its original tenets. Founded by Siddhartha Gautama (c.563–c.483 B.C.), the son of a king in northern India, Buddhism came on the scene at about the same time that Confucius was prescribing his answers for China's society. The foundation of Buddhist doctrine is that all of life is suffering, and that the source of suffering is desire. Consequently, the teachings of Siddhartha Gautama, who was renamed the Enlightened One, or the Buddha, centered on how to remove selfish desire from human nature. To spread his message, the Buddha taught in India's coastal towns because he knew that merchants would take this message across the seas. The ultimate goal in orthodox Buddhism, also known as Therevada Buddhism, is to get off the cycle of birth and rebirth. This happens when one accrues enough good karma (merit) to escape the pain of existence.

The unorthodox forms of this faith found a home in Japan. The more flexible sects of Buddhism were more easily adopted in Japan because indigenous beliefs were combined with these Buddhist variations. As discussed in a following section, several sects became the prominent forms of Buddhism in Japan. Their effects on Japan's society and political landscape were tremendous.

Legalism and the Constitution

"Punish that which is evil and encourage that which is good. This is an excellent rule from antiquity." These words, which introduce the sixth article of the constitution, reflect another Chinese philosophical school that Prince Shōtoku integrated into Japan's political system. It is known as legalism.

Confucius' teachings did not produce unity in China. States continued to battle each other, and war was constantly destroying people's lives. If there was one thing that became clear to the various competing leaders, it was that people were not naturally virtuous. No matter how much philosophy was instilled into people's minds, it did not stop them from hating and killing each other. It was also evident that unless some change was made, the rich would grow richer and more powerful while the poor would sink further into destitution. Chinese thinkers concluded that people must be controlled by a strong state where legalism, or very strict laws, would limit senseless crime and exploitation. In short, harsh law is the only thing that can control people because of humanity's perverted nature. The Japanese incorporated this philosophy into their political system.

The Seventeen-Article Constitution integrated Confucian, legalist, and Buddhist teachings. The Japanese were happy to take foreign ideas and contort them to fit them into their world. Though legalism and Confucianism were competing ideals in China, Japan was pleased to take both philosophies and merge them into something that fit Japan's worldview.

The Soga Fall

Not content to merely introduce Chinese ideas in Japan's first constitution, Shōtoku sent Japanese students to China for academic and religious training. Their duty was to absorb Chinese learning and culture and to transmit it to Japan. These missions coincided with the importation of Korean and Chinese Buddhist priests to the Japanese court. The Yamato court took on many traits of Chinese civilization.

However, the Soga clan was on shaky political ground. Its inordinate influence at the court was resented by other leading families, and by relatives of the reigning empress. In 645 an internal palace coup removed the Soga clan from the court. One of the main leaders against the Soga group was Nakatomi no Kamatari, who later founded the Fujiwara family line. This domestic crisis did not diminish the desire for the court to emulate China. In fact, with the new Fujiwara advisors in place, the stage was set for Japan's greatest era of cultural borrowing from China.

This rendering of Mount Fuji in autumn is found in Tokyo's Koga Rekishi Hakubutsukan Museum.

If time travel were possible, it would be enlightening to transport Western students to eighth-century China. They would find Chang'an, China's capital, the world's largest city and the most cosmopolitan area of the day. More than two million people lived in the capital, which included quarters for the Jewish, Muslim, Zoroastrian, Manichaean, and Nestorian Christian groups. When a Chinese empress died, more than sixty ambassadors from around the world attended the funeral. China's reputation as a producer of unparalleled exquisite porcelain grew during this period. This was China's golden age when the entire country was united under the T'ang Dynasty (618–907).

When T'ang China was in its infant years, Japan also underwent political changes. The Soga clan was toppled and new influences at the court suggested that the bent toward Buddhism and Chinese influence might change. However, the grandeur of T'ang China convinced Japanese leaders that their own state's prospects for economic, social, cultural, and political prosperity depended upon its success in incorporating T'ang policies and principles into the Japanese system. For two centuries the Japanese consciously adapted the Chinese pattern in an era known as the Taiko Reform. Hardly any element of Japanese society was not affected by these changes.

Heian Japan
(794–1185)

Emperor/Land/Taxes

Most people in seventh-century Japan spent their time farming. Clan elders were the local authority and the idea of an all-powerful emperor living in a resplendent imperial capital was not the stuff of everyday conversation. The emperor's authority was limited to areas around the capital. Buddhism, the religion adopted by the court, was a faith for the elite who could read the Chinese religious scripts. In short, the imperial system consisting of an emperor who surrounded himself with advisors, aristocratic relatives, and Buddhist teachers was completely irrelevant to most Japanese people. How different this was from the T'ang system where Chang'an was the hub around which the entire empire revolved. It was said that the Chinese emperor heard the cough of every person in the empire. Japan set out to copy China's centralized system. This process began with the elevation of the emperor's position.

According to traditional Chinese cosmology there are three spheres of reality: heaven, earth, and humanity. It was humanity's responsibility to maintain the balance and harmony between heaven and earth. As such, a primary role of Chinese emperors was to offer annual sacrifices to heaven and to act as a mediator between the unseen and seen worlds. Thus, the sovereign was often referred to as "The Son of Heaven." This system granted all authority to the emperor because he was the mediator between heaven and earth. To reject the emperor's command was to ignore the will of heaven. Japan went a step beyond this paradigm. Japanese emperors were not representatives of heaven, they themselves were considered divine.

Japanese chroniclers set out to legitimize the claim of the emperor's divinity through the written word. Eighth-century Japanese historians picked up on China's use of recorded history. History was a key subject for the Chinese because precedent dictated the details surrounding rites and ceremonies. Confucius himself insisted that he was not inventing any new philosophy; rather, he was only transmitting the teachings of ancient Chinese sage kings. Two Japanese historical texts, the *Kojiki* (A.D. 712) and the *Nihon Shoki* (A.D. 720) proved invaluable as a written record of Japan's past. The *Kojiki's* content was a bit more mythical than the later text. Both books, however, traced the emperor's lineage to the sun goddess, Amaterasu. Japanese sovereigns were believed to be the direct descendants of the gods. This doctrine remained in place for more than a thousand years. Even when the Japanese adopted its first modern constitution in 1889, the emperor was described as "sacred and inviolable."

Since the Japanese regarded the emperor as a god, it was natural that all things belonged to him. Using this rationale, the ruler's advisors claimed that all Japan's land belonged to the emperor. As such, he had the right to tax it. Farmers, who also belonged to the emperor, were told that they were privileged to cultivate the ruler's land. Land surveys allowed the court to determine the expected revenue.

Using the T'ang model, the Japanese instituted a new system of political titles. The establishment of eight ministries assisted in the governance of the state. These branches of government included the Imperial House Ministry, Finance Ministry, Ministry of People's Affairs, War Ministry, Ceremony Ministry, Central Affairs Ministry, Military Affairs, and the Justice Ministry. In addition to these political changes, the emperor appointed provincial governors, which replaced the outmoded clan system. Japan was growing up.

A Capital for an Emperor

During the earliest reigns of the Yamato kings, the imperial family's location changed every time a ruler died. These moves were based on the belief that the sovereign's death polluted the region. The various tombs noted in an earlier section indicate that after a king's death the family moved to a new region where they would dwell until the next king passed away. The T'ang system convinced the Yamato leaders that a permanent capital was more useful. The natural choice for a political center was an area now known as Nara.

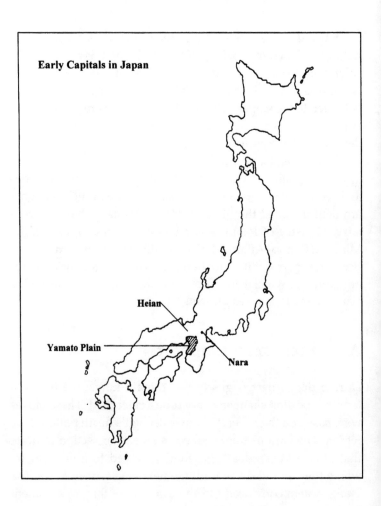

Early Capitals in Japan

Heian

Yamato Plain

Nara

Located on the Yamato Plain, Nara, formerly known as Heijo, was where Japan's first Buddhist temples were erected. In 710 the court constructed a checkerboard layout of a 2.5 by 3 mile zone in Nara and proceeded to build a city in the image of Chang'an. The project was overly ambitious. The Japanese did not have the requisite population and resources to create an imposing capital. High surrounding walls, which characterized Chang'an, were not part of the Nara architecture. In fact, the western portion of the city was never fully constructed before the government decided to move the capital to a location thirty miles away in 784.

After this false start, the new Nara capital was established in 794. This location was named Heian-kyō (later known as Kyoto). Some historians speculate that the reason for the imperial move was to break free from the influences of the numerous Buddhist sects that had grown in the region. The new capital, similar in style to Nara, was larger in scale than anything Japan had built to date. Emperor Kemmu (r. 781–806) took unprecedented control of the government and directed the plans for the resettlement of his headquarters. Heian remained the imperial capital until 1868, and the grandeur of Kyoto became the pride of the Japanese people.

Japan on Its Own

To whom do you turn after you've learned everything you can from a particular teacher? Japan was confronted with this

This is a roof ridge-end tile from the Nara period.

question during the 800s. For a good number of reasons T'ang China was no longer appealing to the Japanese. Rather than turn to another tutor, Japan turned in on itself. Japan's growing disenchantment with China was partly due to the decline of the T'ang political system. During the ninth century, Chinese society crumbled as an ineffective T'ang bureaucracy seemed unable to make needed changes. Japan went in another direction.

Another cause for Japan's turn away from China was that Japan never quite caught on to the Chinese idea of a merit-based bureaucracy. China believed that the empire's brightest minds should govern the state. More than one hundred years before Christ, the Chinese established a system wherein candidates for political office took exams to prove their intellectual abilities. These exams became even more elaborate and sophisticated during T'ang China. Every year hopeful applicants for government posts took these state-sponsored exams. Only the brightest passed these tests. Thus, China tapped the most intellectually gifted men to serve in the bureaucratic network. The content of these assessment exercises was ancient Chinese texts.

Japan tried to emulate this pattern, even to the point of setting up an imperial academy to prepare students for the tests. But in Japan the examination system and the open invitation to join the bureaucracy did not work. Japan's imperial court with its numerous emperor-related clans and a pattern of nepotism meant that government positions were handed down from father to son. Political and economic power grew around the Heian capital, and an aristocratic bureaucracy emerged.

Finally, two related issues sealed the fate of Japan's independence from the Chinese model: the growth of private property and the rise of a military class. These two issues were so volatile that they led to a bloody civil war, the emergence of the shogunate, and five hundred years of feudalism.

The *Shoen* (Estate) System

Following T'ang China's example, seventh- and eighth-century Japanese bureaucrats completed thorough land surveys through which Japan was divided into sixty-six provinces. Breaking this division down even further, provinces were partitioned into counties and then villages. Land surveys were based on the assumptions that all of Japan belonged to the emperor and a percentage of all yields should be returned to the sovereign. Revenue that flowed into Kyoto provided the funds for the luxurious lifestyle of a growing aristocracy.

In theory, this system was supposed to create a strong central government with a populace content to pay taxes while enjoying a stable source of food. However, a weak link in the system actually served to destabilize all of Japan. The economic flaw was that portions of Japan were designated tax-free zones. These restricted areas included the properties on which Buddhist monasteries were built, areas immediately adjacent to Shinto shrines, areas of land reclamation, and small land grants that the emperor bestowed to an individual or family as gifts for a service previously rendered. Initially these tax-free lands were negligible. This changed during the ninth and tenth centuries, when Buddhist monasteries grew in size and influence. Consequently, more land was needed to sustain thousands of monks. The more prosperous farmers and nobles also gained tax-free land by hiring laborers for reclamation projects. Moreover, the small land grant gifts also increased in size. The story behind this latter growth testifies to early Japanese entrepreneurial efforts. Owners of revenue-free land approached adjacent homes and villages with an enticing offer: "Join your land to ours and you too can enjoy tax-free status." The primary motive for accepting this offer was the promise that fewer crops would be owed to landowners than were due to the emperor. Also, gangs increasingly harassed farmers because decreased state revenue made it difficult for the court to provide protection for the farmers. The owners of large tax-free properties promised protection for any plowman who joined his property to the estate (*shoen*).

This absconding of public land continued until the eleventh century when 50 percent of Japan's agrarian land belonged to private properties. Of course the loser in all of this was the imperial house. Every year tax returns diminished. The emperor and his advisors found it increasingly difficult to maintain a stable state due to the steady decrease of resources. Responding to the growing economic crisis, the court initiated an updated land survey.

Many *shoen* owners who clandestinely increased their land holdings knew that this new inspection would, at the very least, cause them embarrassment or, at worse, cost them their very lives. They had grown wealthy at the state's expense. Worse still, they had reciprocated an emperor's generosity by illegally adding state land to their tax-free zones. To avoid catastrophe, *shoen* owners formed alliances with various influential Kyoto families. The *quid pro quo* arrangement worked as follows: *shoen* proprietors siphoned some of their profits to Kyoto aristocrats. In return, these nobles instructed the inspectors to bypass the regions where the landowners were filtering money to Kyoto. Members of the imperial family were also involved in this ruse. It was, however, the Fujiwara house (the family from which the emperors took their brides) that profited the most from this scheme.

The Rise of the Military Class

The military is one prominent thread that runs through the tapestry of Japanese history and was at the forefront of Japan's political, economic, and social systems until 1945. The terms "samurai" and "shogun" are familiar throughout the world. It is helpful to understand how this class emerged and subsequently dominated Japan.

When Japan moved toward the T'ang centralized government scheme, it instituted universal conscription so that men regularly provided free labor for the emperor. Their tasks might include building bridges, carrying equipment or rice, or acting as constables for the Kyoto court. At the local level, conscripts were tasked to police their respective towns. Thus, provincial

This is a copy of the elaborate armor worn by Japanese soldiers in the twelfth century.

officials used universal conscriptions to insure local security, though there was minimal rural disturbance during the eighth century. At any rate, policing in eighth-century Japan required minimal skill and time expenditure.

During the eighth century, the Emishi, a minority group in eastern Japan, came into conflict with the Japanese. Exactly who the Emishi were is a continuing debate, though it is probable that they were related to the Ainu peoples. Initial battles between the conscripts and the Emishi proved disastrous for the Japanese. To drive the Emishi further north, the Japanese needed an armor-wearing cavalry equipped with the latest weaponry. Common farmers would face economic disaster if they tried to equip their sons with such regalia because armor was prohibitively expensive. Thus, the Japanese horse-riding soldiers that displaced the Emishi came from the economically affluent class.

At approximately the same time, changes in the police force occurred at Kyoto and the southern island of Kyushu. Young men from wealthy families purchased armor and, when available, horses. Identified as *saburai* (private retainer), these professional soldiers guarded the emperor, roamed Kyushu, and traveled east to take on the Emishi. The term *saburai* was later changed to samurai.

During the ninth and tenth centuries the role of the samurai dramatically changed. Increased lawlessness and the resultant decrease in the emperor's ability to respond to crises created a field day for roaming brigands. Responding to this growing chaos, *shoen* proprietors turned to prominent samurai for protection. These military leaders, accompanied by their retainers, protected the *shoen* property and its inhabitants. Indeed, many estate owners moved to Kyoto and left the management of their estates to the samurai.

Because the samurai came from an elite class, great prestige was attached to the military group. Nonetheless, for the first centuries of their existence, the samurai were more akin to mercenaries than to soldiers loyal to a cause or leader. The notion of intense loyalty was attached later through the adoption of the warrior code (*bushido*).

Heian Culture

With money and rich landlords pouring into Kyoto, an atmosphere of luxury blossomed at the capital. Of course, all of this private opulence was at the expense of shrinking state revenues. The true nature of wealth and power in Kyoto was evidenced in the urban architecture. While the imperial compound and other state buildings fell into disrepair due to negligence and lack of funds, the *shoen* proprietors and the sponsors of rural estates lived in the finest quarters. Kyoto's national university, once the pride of the capital, was reduced to a corrupt organization filled with disinterested scholars.

Culture among the Heian affluent reflected lavish lifestyles as silk was the preferred material for clothing. A woman's beauty was more closely tied to her hair and dress than it was to her face. Since most wealthy women painted white chalk on

The cult of the sword is best explained as an emotional attachment a soldier felt with his weapon.

their faces, applied rouge to their cheeks, and blackened their teeth, more attention was directed to the length and thickness of a woman's hair than to her facial features. Men wore silk robes and were judged by their social gracefulness and their wardrobes rather than their physical attributes.

This was also the period when Japanese writing began to surpass the traditional Chinese literature. Japanese poetry graduated to lengthier diaries and novels written in the indigenous style. The most famous novel of the period is *The Tale of Genji*. Written by Murasaki Shikibu (c.978–c.1026), a woman at court, this novel follows the fictitious adventures of Genji, the son of an emperor. Low in action and yet rich in the intricate details of court life, the novel describes Heian court protocol and amorous secret meetings between lovers.

Japanese novels were surprisingly numerous during the early Heian years, demonstrating that there was ample opportunity to read and write. Some believe that this free time was a result of human lethargy brought on by a poor diet. Meat and fat were missing from the regular diet of the Japanese elite. Buddhism, with its emphasis on preserving all life, along with a limited supply of meat, contributed to the absence of these products among the Heian nobles. While fish added protein to the Japanese diet, lack of refrigeration necessitated that merchants sell dried fish. Apart from water, the only other drink noted in Heian times was rice wine (sake). Though low in alcohol content, it easily inebriated those that drank it.

Civil War and the Rise of the Shogunate

Revenue shortfalls resulted in the court's inability to maintain any semblance of order throughout the land. Rural residents as well as those who had financial stakes in the *shoen* system were naturally drawn to the strongest samurai families. Two of these families, the Minamoto and Taira houses, were related to the nobles in Kyoto. Minamoto and Taira's influence and power radically increased in the rural regions.

At the court these military houses aligned on opposing sides with the two competing families: the imperial line and the Fujiwara house. As noted earlier, the Fujiwara house was intricately involved with court politics because it was the clan from which the emperors chose their brides. It was also Kyoto's richest family because of its complicity in absconding state land. As relations between the Fujiwara and imperial houses deteriorated, outside alliances were sought and formed. A civil war broke out in 1156 pitting the imperial/Taira houses against the alliance of the Fujiwara/Minamoto houses. The imperial/Taira coalition won this four-year bloody war. Unfortunately for the victors, Taira Kiyomori (1118–81), the leader of the victorious armies, made two postwar errors. First, he moved to the capital and indulged in the same luxurious lifestyle that had contributed to the fall of his enemies. Second, he allowed Yoritomo, a young prince from the Minamoto house, to survive. Yoritomo was raised by the Hōjō clan, a collateral family of the Taira house. As he grew into manhood, the charismatic Yoritomo drew disgruntled samurai to himself. He

formed alliances based on the promise that land would be allocated to the victorious generals. His forces grew to such an
extent that in 1183 Yoritomo's army attacked and captured
Kyoto. Yoritomo defeated Taira Kiyomori and the course of
Japan's history was forever changed.

THE SHOGUN CAPITALS

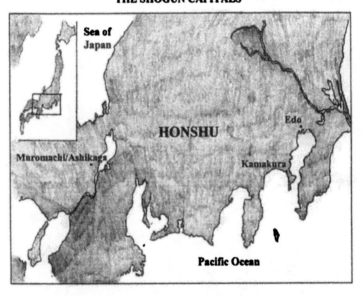

Shogun Rule in Japan
(1192–1868)

The Kamakura *Bakufu* (1192–1333)

Yoritomo's post-victory policies were brilliant. Rather than accepting an empty bureaucratic title, he accepted the title of *seii taishogun* (leading barbarian-suppressing general). This title, as all other official ones, had to be bestowed by the emperor. Certainly Yoritomo had the military backing to call himself Japan's generalissimo, but protocol dictated that he wait for the court to bestow upon him the title of shogun. Given his military victories, Yoritomo only had to wait until 1192 when the intimidated court gave him the coveted title.

Yoritomo also deviated from past political policy and declared that he would not live in Kyoto. He correctly surmised that every time leaders moved to Kyoto they became soft bureaucrats, falling into the seductive lap of luxury. Thus, a second capital to house the shogun was created at Kamakura on the Kanto Plain. The two-capital system remained in place until 1869 with Kyoto remaining the imperial capital while the shogun's city of residence, called the *bakufu* or the "tent government" moved according to the whims of each shogun that rose to power. While ceremonial power resided in Kyoto, the real power for more than six centuries was at the *bakufu*. From 1185 to 1868 the three *bakufu* areas were Kamakura (1185–1333), Muromachi (1333–1573), and Edo (1603–1868).

Yoritomo also promoted his leading generals to provincial constables. These military leaders were called *shugo*. The *shugo* deputies who were direct managers of the land were called *jito*. The *shoen* system remained intact and the *bakufu* was responsible for keeping the peace on all the estates as well as the remaining state-owned land.

Headquartered on Japan's largest stretch of flat land, the 120-mile Kanto Plain, the Kamakura *bakufu* was the shortest-lasting of the three military reigns in Japan. In fact, it is quite remarkable that it lasted as long as it did given the continual crises it endured.

Hōjō Power

Yoritomo's leadership provided stability during the early Kamakura years. His death, however, created the first major *bakufu* emergency. Though Yoritomo had two sons to carry on the Minamoto rule, his Hōjō in-laws, with the aid of Yoritomo's wife, eliminated the two boys and placed a Hōjō-approved candidate as the next shogun. Hōjō elders dominated the shogun for the remainder of the Kamakura era. Similarly, the emperor was dominated by retired emperors and regents. Provincial governors concluded Japan's entire authority paradigm was a sham. They argued that if the emperor and shogun were just puppets of behind-the-scenes power brokers, then loyalty was not due to the throne or *bakufu*. Rebels against the court and the *bakufu* used this argument to legitimize their disobedience.

Mongol Invasions

Foreign pressures added to the domestic woes that Kamakura officials faced. In the early 1260s, Kublai Khan, the grandson of the great Mongol unifier, Genghis Khan, rallied his army and established his new capital at Peking. China was now under the sway of a foreign ruler. Kublai Khan intended to force Korea and Japan to submit to Mongol hegemony. In his initial letters to Japan's imperial court, the Mongol sovereign indicated that Heaven had given him the mandate to rule over the earth. Moreover, Korea had already submitted and reportedly was pleased with their new relation to China. The letter ended with a promise and a veiled threat. The assurance was that the Mongols did not wish to conquer Japan; they merely wanted to receive the respect due them. The warning was that "Nobody would wish to resort to arms."

This initial correspondence did not reach Japan because Korean ambassadors, the intermediaries used by Kublai Khan, were afraid to present it to the Japanese. Subsequent dispatches went unheeded as the *shugo* on Tsushima, an island between Korea and Japan, drove off those that brought the khan's overtures. Eventually, however, the letter reached the Japanese emperor. Japan did not respond to it for several reasons. First, Japan had been somewhat isolated since the tenth century and had minimal diplomatic history. Corresponding with an individual claiming to be the ruler of the universe was a new experience for Japan. What type of tribute was required for the khan? What type of ambassadors should be sent? How many? Rather than becoming tangled in a web of sticky diplomacy, Japan chose the path of silence. Moreover, the khan had sent the dispatch to the wrong address. Assuming that power rested at the imperial court, messages were sent to Kyoto rather than to Kamakura. It was said that the emperor could not sneeze without asking the *bakufu*'s permission, so it was highly unlikely that the court would act alone on such an important matter. Finally, the Japanese possessed limited information on the Mongols. The knowledge that they did possess about the Mongols came from two groups: the Chinese, who were fleeing for their lives, and Korean Buddhist priests. Both groups only had negative things to say about the Mongols.

Frustrated by Japan's lack of response, Kublai Khan ordered an attack on Japan by a joint Mongol and Korean force. These soldiers were armed with the most advanced military technologies. Bombs and poisoned arrows were used against the Japanese. The *bakufu* ordered the Kyushu *shugo* to defend the shores of Japan, as Kyushu was the island closest to the Korean Peninsula and was the area attacked by the Mongols. Despite the bravery of the Japanese, the Mongol forces gained the upper hand in capturing islands close to Kyushu. However, due to the change of seasons, the khan's forces returned to Korea before the pivotal battle for Kyushu. Strong typhoons plague the shores of Kyushu during hurricane season and the Mongols did not want to lose their ships to the boisterous sea.

Having demonstrated military superiority, the Mongols returned to diplomacy. Mongol ambassadors arrived in Japan, and this time they traveled to the *bakufu* rather than Kyoto. Nonetheless the result was the same. Japan refused the Mongol overtures. Some historians write that Japan's answer to the repeated diplomatic missions was to decapitate the Mongol ambassadors and send their heads back to the khan's court. Such hubris was too much for the Mongol leader and he ordered that thousands of ships be gathered for a massive invasion.

For its part, the Kamakura *bakufu* was proactive in its anticipation of the khan's wrath. Samurai from around Japan were instructed to transfer to Kyoto. The *bakufu* ordered the construction of a wall along the shores of Kyushu, the dimensions of which were fifteen miles long, twelve feet high, and thirteen feet wide. Aristocrats, shugo, and the *jito* responded to this crisis by providing the *bakufu* with unprecedented economic and military support.

In 1281 a Mongol force of 4,400 ships and 157,000 men set out to conquer Japan. It was the world's largest marine force to date. Once again the Mongols enjoyed initial success due to their technological superiority. However, before the invaders' final advance, an unexpected typhoon struck the Mongol fleet, destroying a good portion of it. Casualties numbered in the tens of thousands, and the Mongols limped back to Korea, never again to seriously threaten Japan. Japan attributed its unlikely victory—against an army that had yet to be stopped by any other Asian nation—to heavenly providence, what is more commonly known as the *kamikaze*, The Divine Wind. This reinforced Japan's notion that it was invincible. As the children of the gods, there was no way their deities would let them lose in a foreign war. It was a notion that was perpetuated when Japan surprised the world with its military victories over China in 1895 and against Imperial Russia in 1905.

One might conclude that the *bakufu*'s glorious victory over the Mongols added legitimacy to the Hōjō rule. However, following this victory there were many disgruntled Japanese: the *shugo* were offended that so much was asked of them with no tangible rewards; farmers complained about inordinate taxation due to the war; and the imperial court resented the growing encroachment of the *bakufu*'s influence. In fact, the *bakufu* inserted itself into court politics because of the bitter rivalries within the imperial family. As noted earlier, regents and retired emperors remained the force behind the reigning emperor. However, succession to the throne became tricky because of the *bakufu*'s unwanted meddling. The imperial family was so divided that the two primary family branches alternately placed their sons on the throne.

Emperor Go-Daigo (1288–1339)

One strong-willed emperor upset this system; he was the ninety-sixth emperor of Japan, Go-Daigo (1288–1339). In 1318 he ascended to the throne and consolidated his power by disallowing interference from retired emperors. Go-Daigo also insisted that taxes from local lands and breweries make their way to the imperial house. Land surveys were updated so more taxes would flow into Kyoto. These actions encroached on *bakufu* authority and angered the shogun's advisors. *Bakufu* leaders insisted that Go-Daigo abdicate in favor of a more pliable candidate, but he refused to step down.

The Kamakura *bakufu* lost patience with Go-Daigo and ordered one of its generals, Takauji of the Ashikaga house, to march against the imperial house, put down the rebellion, and install an emperor who would obey the *bakufu*. Takauji marched on Kyoto, but in a surprising twist he aligned with Emperor Go-Daigo and supported the rebellion against the *bakufu*. Unable to hold its territory on the Kanto Plain, the Kamakura *bakufu* came to an end in 1333.

No longer restrained by the *bakufu*, Emperor Go-Daigo announced the establishment of the Kemmu Restoration (1333–1336). This short-lived movement placed state authority in the hands of the emperor. The entire *shoen* system was reconsidered with the intention of reverting to a plan where Japan's land, and all its accompanying taxes, belonged to the emperor.

Go-Daigo is considered a tragic hero in Japan's history. He is revered because he advocated the supremacy of the emperor, which is tied to the legend of Amaterasu and the divine nature of Japan's ruler and land. He is labeled tragic because he was not politically astute enough to maintain his position. The alliance between Go-Daigo and Ashikaga Takauji broke down. One point of contention was that samurai were disgruntled by the meager monetary compensation allocated to them from the emperor. Moreover, Takauji moved to Kyoto to accept the new mantle of power as Japan's new shogun. Despite lobbying for this title, Go-Daigo refused to appoint Takauji to the position of shogun, choosing rather to appoint a candidate who was more susceptible to court influence. The emperor also appointed nobles to replace the *shugo* as district administrators.

Takauji turned against the emperor and Go-Daigo fled the capital, taking with him the imperial regalia. He set up his headquarters in the Yoshino Mountains that are south of the Nara Plain. Rather than pursuing Go-Daigo, Takauji installed a prince from the imperial house as the new emperor. Between 1336 and 1392 there were two imperial courts in Japan, both claiming legitimacy. Eventually, the Kyoto group emerged victorious in the bloodless rivalry between the "North" and "South" emperors.

Takauji was named shogun by the emperor he enthroned. The Ashikaga house moved its capital to a suburb of Kyoto known as Muromachi. The period from 1338 to 1573 is known as the Ashikaga, or Muromachi era.

Muromachi Japan (1338–1573)

Takauji's decision to station the *bakufu* at the outskirts of Kyoto carried with it both advantages and drawbacks. By its geographic proximity to the imperial court, the *bakufu* kept close tabs on nobles and emperors. It was also easier for the Japanese to recognize one geographical area from which authority was handed down. Yet these benefits were far surpassed by the disadvantages of locating the *bakufu* close to the imperial capital. For example, the Ashikaga house could not control much of Japan outside of the areas immediately surrounding Kyoto. During Kamakura days, the shogun lived on Japan's largest plain and surveyed the machinations of various *shugo*, nobles, and the rank-and-file farmers. In Kyoto, the *bakufu* also was influenced heavily by numerous Buddhist temples and sects that dotted the capital's landscape. The Muromachi shoguns became more enamored with art and culture than the Kamakura shoguns had been. The result was the softening of the militaristic side of the shogun. These disadvantages would eventually lead to the demise of the Muromachi shogunate.

Medieval Culture in Japan

Despite the political disarray during Kamakura and Muromachi Japan, there were aspects of culture that flowered throughout the islands. Japan came out of its cocoon and stretched its wings during this period only to once again return to an even stricter isolation that was eventually disturbed by American warships.

Much of the cultural growth in Japan during the first two shogunates was due to the emergence of new Buddhist sects. The first of these centered on the Buddha Amida and the doctrine that salvation was possible for all people. Some Buddhists ascribe to the doctrine that there are epochs when Buddhist law is disregarded and forgotten. For the medieval Japanese who ascribed to this belief, the hedonism in Kyoto and the increased exploitation of farmers was evidence that a dark age had fallen upon Japan. It was within this context that the rise of the Amida doctrine became popular. The first Amida sect was called the Pure Land (Jōdo) Faith. This somewhat anti-establishment arm of Buddhism was brought to Japan from China and was spread through the teachings of the popular priest, Hōnen (1133–1212).

This twelfth-century Buddhist statue represents the Buddha Amida or the Buddha whose righteousness saves all those who place their faith in him.

In the Pure Land doctrine, salvation came through the right-eousness of another, the Buddha Amida. One achieved this enlightenment by repeatedly calling on the name of Buddha Amida and placing one's hope on the good works of Amida. Shinran, a disciple of Hōnen, made the attainment of salvation even easier. According to Shinran, a person only had to call on the name of Amida one time, and he or she would be saved. His sect became known as the True Pure Land (Jōdo Shinshū). These popular forms of Buddhism broke down the wall between the clerics and the common people. Salvation was possible even for those who could not read the Buddhist scriptures. Shinran demonstrated his abandonment of the traditional monastery and celibacy vows by marrying a female acquaintance.

From a cultural standpoint, Zen Buddhism had the greatest impact on Japan during the Kamakura and Ashikaga shogu-nates. Brought to Japan from China, this sect appealed to the shogun and the samurai class. What was emphasized in this faith was enlightenment through meditation. The two main subjects for Zen contemplation were esoteric questions (what is the sound of one hand clapping?) and questions regarding the reality of the universe. One could learn the disciplines of a con-templative life by becoming a disciple of a more accomplished monk. The preeminent masters that the Japanese Zen followers attached themselves to were from China. This exposed Japanese culture to all things Chinese. Artwork, literature, and crafts from China became highly valued in Japan, and one's prestige was connected to the accumulation of Chinese art. Also, during the Ashikaga shogunate, trade between China and Japan increased Zen Buddhism's influence in Japan.

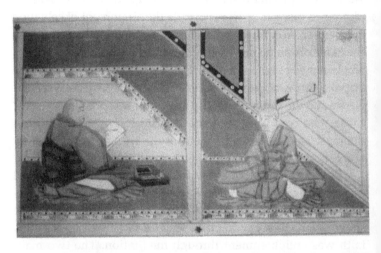

In this fourteenth-century illustrated biography of a priest, the master is teaching the student how to prepare for rebirth in the Pure Land.

This is a representation of a fourteenth-century Buddhist priest.

Zen Buddhists also emphasized the simple over the complex, the natural over the invented, and the elegant over the massive. Bonsai trees, flower arrangements, and ordered gardens became part of Japan's culture during this period. Tea drinking evolved from a practice of the elite, to a competitive test-tasting contest, to a ceremony requiring detailed etiquette.

As Buddhism increased in popularity so too did a type of medieval literature in Japan that became known as the war epic. These literary accounts focused on the rise and fall of the Taira house. Legendary battles were meticulously recounted and former military figures became famous because of this literature. This literary material was the subject for another new cultural phenomenon in medieval Japan—the Noh play.

The precursor to the Noh play was an entertainment troupe that traveled across Japan. Performances included juggling acts, dances, and acrobatic feats. A more sophisticated act, the Noh developed where actors reenacted historical events. A narrator or chorus was located on the side of the stage while masked characters acted out the story. The Noh drama became a fixture of Japanese culture.

The Warring States Period

The peak of Ashikaga influence in Japan occurred during the 1368 to 1394 reign of Ashikaga Yoshimitsu (1358–1408). Under his rule the two rival imperial houses were reunited. Yoshimitsu advocated the cultural development of the military class. He became a refined, sophisticated, and cultured leader. A

This mask used in Noh plays is entitled "The Liar."

A Noh mask that is used to represent a woman.

A Noh mask of a fox.

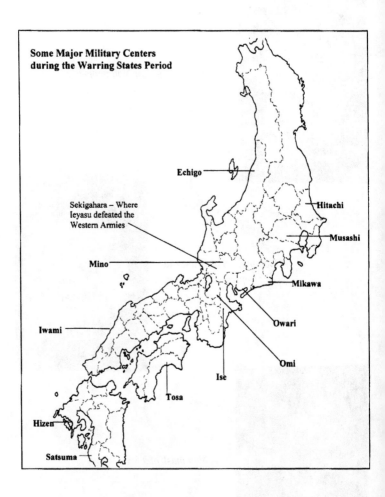

Some Major Military Centers during the Warring States Period

Echigo

Hitachi

Sekigahara – Where Ieyasu defeated the Western Armies

Musashi

Mino

Mikawa

Iwami

Owari

Omi

Ise

Tosa

Hizen

Satsuma

primary patron of the arts, Yoshimitsu encouraged all military leaders to devote their energies to cultural refinement.

The Ashikaga shoguns, however, never controlled all of Japan. Their close proximity to Kyoto hindered their effectiveness as protectors of distant provinces. In fact, the Ashikaga *bakufu* had to walk a very thin tightrope. Its land base was not extensive, and it had few personal ties with the *shugo* and the *jito*. To cultivate the support of these groups, the shogun expanded the powers of the *shugo* to include civil as well as military authority throughout the provinces. They became the judicial leaders of the land, and they also collected taxes.

The area that each *shugo* governed often resembled a patchwork of disjointed lands rather than a single geographic region. Because land was divided according to decrees from Kyoto, the military governors competed for the landed aristocrats' allegiance. These nobles would serve as *shugo* lobbyists to the emperor who confirmed each *shugo's* right to rule certain territories.

During the fourteenth and fifteenth centuries, a subtle but significant shift occurred throughout Japan. As the *shugo's* power increased, it became apparent that the shift in authority was complete. The obvious issue was that if the *shugo* collected taxes, ruled in judicial classes, and acted as the civil authority, then what was to stop them from disregarding the authority of a relatively weak shogun or lazy aristocrats? Realizing this dangerous shift in authority, the *bakufu* responded by overextending the responsibilities of the *shugo*. It made sure that the *shugo* were forced to govern wide geographical areas to diffuse potential rivals. The major implication of this action was that the *shugo* became more reliant on their samurai deputies, the *jito*. This shift changed Japan.

This delicate balance of power unraveled in 1467. During that year a quarrel over who should be the next shogun spilled over to the *shugo*. Alliances for each claimant marched into Kyoto and for ten years the capital of peace and tranquility was more akin to a bloody war zone. *Shugo* took this specter of lawlessness as a cue to overthrow any form of shogunal authority. More significantly, the *jito* created autonomous zones and declared their independence from the *shugo*. In 1467 there were thirty *shugo;* ten years later only a dozen remained in power. Consequently, Japan was carved into numerous petty states where the right to rule was based on who held the most military power. Heaven's mandate, the emperor's blessing, and the shogun's authority were irrelevant to the autonomous *jito* and *shugo*.

There were significant reasons why the *bakufu* and emperor lost social and political prestige. Between 1467 and 1550, three of the five appointed shoguns were exiled, one died in battle, and the fifth was assassinated. Ashikaga's land holdings dwindled from 250 regions to 34. Things were not much better for the imperial house. During the first half of the sixteenth century Emperor Go Hashiwabara had to wait twenty-one years to be enthroned because there was not enough money to have a proper enthronement ceremony. Other emperors were reduced to selling their calligraphy for much-needed funds.

Yet, despite these hard times, the imperial system did not pass from the scene. The social presupposition was that political legitimacy had to come from the emperor. Although the capital was weak, more than forty *jito* requested appointment as *shugo* after 1500. Despite having military power, most *jito* and *shugo* acknowledged that they needed imperial approval for a proper rule.

The one-hundred-year period between 1450 and 1550 in Japan is referred to as the era of Warring States. Japanese chroniclers borrowed this title from an earlier time in China when civil war crippled the Middle Kingdom. The Japanese also refer to the Warring States period as *gekokujo jidai* or the "mastery of the high by the low." But from the ashes of political chaos, three successive military leaders emerged to reunify Japan. Before describing the contributions of these men, it is important to note two sixteenth-century changes in Japan's architectural and religious realms—the castle and the European Catholic priests.

At the outset of the Warring States era, *jito* and *shugo* enlisted farmers to fight, and as regional forces grew in size, defenses did as well. Military leaders responded to enormous armies by building large castles for defensive purposes. These new edifices included moats and decorative architecture. Many castles still remain intact, and they are reminders of Japan's past.

Castles were also built in response to the growing use of guns—weapons that were introduced to the Japanese by the Portuguese. During the first decades of the sixteenth century Portuguese and Spanish ships made their way to Asia in search of the coveted Spice Islands. The Portuguese established their headquarters at the port town of Malacca on the southern tip of the Malaya Peninsula. From this port, they made their way to Japan. In 1543 the first Portuguese reached the islands off the coast of Kyushu. Two years later regular trade was established

From the Warring States Period, this black tea bowl was formed only by hand—no wheel was used. The quiet form reflects the deep spirituality associated with the tea ceremony.

Fifteenth-century civil war led to the construction of numerous castles for defensive purposes. This is the Koga Castle in today's Ibaraki Prefecture in central Honshu.

between the Europeans and the Japanese. As this was the time of civil strife in Japan, the primary motive for the Japanese befriending the Europeans was to acquire modern weaponry.

The most influential westerners to enter Japan during the sixteenth century were the Catholic priests. In 1549, Francis Xavier (1506–1552) a leading figure in the newly created Jesuit order of the Roman Catholic Church, came to Japan. He was unsuccessful in his attempts to convert the emperor and shogun, but there were some leading military figures that responded positively to Xavier's message. In fact, military chiefs gave the priests the village of Nagasaki and built a large cathedral in the port community. In return, the Japanese insisted that the clerics pressure the European traders to exclusively trade with certain Japanese *shugo* and *jito*. The Christian missionaries in Japan were quite successful in their proselytizing efforts during the sixteenth century. However, their efforts were severely curtailed once Japan became politically united. It is to that process of unification that we now turn our attention.

Japan's Three Unifiers

A Japanese saying regarding the three men who unified Japan is: "Oda Nobunaga kneaded the dough; Toyotomi Hideyoshi baked the bread; and Tokugawa Ieyasu ate the loaf." These three men were instrumental in setting Japan onto the path of unity and modernity. Each one left a stronger Japan for his successor to build on.

Oda Nobunaga (1534–1582)

Oda Nobunaga was born into a very troubled world. His father was one of several *jito* in Owari. Though Owari was relatively small, with only eight districts, it was geographically important as it was attached to the larger domains of Mikawa, Mino, and Ise. Its soil was extremely fertile and farmers in Owari were fortunate to be able to work such good land. In 1551, upon the death of Oda Nobunaga's father, the son began consolidating power and took up arms against those who rejected his rule in Owari. In 1562, Nobunaga had complete control of his province and had made a strategic alliance with Tokugawa Ieyasu, the dominant leader of Mikawa.

Having grown in power and prestige, Nobunaga marched into Kyoto in 1568. Once established in Kyoto, Nobunaga had the emperor proclaim Ashikaga Yoshiaki the new shogun. Nobunaga believed that he could dominate Yoshiaki, but the alliance quickly broke down. Though Yoshiaki knew he owed his position to Nobunaga, the new shogun would be nobody's puppet. His open rebellion caused Nobunaga to stamp out the Ashikaga shogunate, thus ending the second military rule of Japan.

Nobunaga believed that power legitimized itself. His ruthless destruction of Buddhist monasteries and any group that stood in his way made him feared throughout the Kyoto area. He had ten generals under his leadership, including his old ally Tokugawa Ieyasu.

Having defeated the powerful forces of Omi province, Nobunaga built his castle at Azuchi, a district on the east side of Lake Biwa. He continued to spread his influence with an eye toward reuniting Japan. In mid-1582 he traveled to Kyoto to entertain some of the emperor's advisors. During Nobunaga's visit to the capital, one of his disgruntled generals quietly entered Kyoto and assassinated him.

Even though Nobunaga began the process of reunifying Japan, he is reviled in Japanese history. A script from an eighteenth-century Japanese play actually proclaims his assassin as a hero: "Heedless of remonstrations, Nobunaga destroyed shrines and temples, daily piling up atrocity upon atrocity. It was my calling to slay him for the sake of the Warrior's Way, for the sake of the realm. King Wu slew King Chou of the Yin; Hōjō Yoshitoki exiled the emperor. Both in our country and China, the murder of a lord who does not know the Way has been the task of great men who thus give relief to the people." The reason Nobunaga is somewhat despised is that he reportedly did not follow the way of harmony.

Toyotomi Hideyoshi (1536–1598)

Following Nobunaga's assassination, a scramble for power brought a rather unlikely figure to the forefront of Japan. Toyotomi Hideyoshi, one of Nobunaga's ten generals, was from a farming family in Owari Province. He had little to boast about. He had a rather weak physical constitution, and he was homely: Nobunaga once described Hideyoshi as looking like a bald rat. Nonetheless, he was an expert at diplomacy. While Nobunaga used military might to gain victory, Hideyoshi preferred to make peace while sipping tea with an adversary.

This 1918 painting of Toyotomi Hideyoshi is from the artist, Shimomura Kanzen (1873–1930).

His policy of diplomacy was extremely successful. He did not have a military campaign that lasted more than six months. Within eight years of Nobunaga's death, all of Japan became united under Hideyoshi. One policy that brought peace to Japan was a 1588 law that required all non-military personnel to surrender their weapons. Farmers returned to tilling the soil full-time. By law, only the samurai could carry a sword. Three years later Hideyoshi froze Japan's social order. Samurai were forced to move off of farmland and into castle towns. Farmers were commanded to remain in their occupations. Extensive and detailed land surveys gave Hideyoshi the information he needed to properly tax all of Japan. Land was measured by the number of *koku* (five bushels) it could produce. Hideyoshi transferred his military leaders to various provinces to ensure the maintenance of proper social and economic order. He also held the power to relocate these military leaders when and where he wanted. Hideyoshi transferred his main competitor, Tokugawa Ieyasu, to eastern Japan where he settled in the small fishing village of Edo. Ieyasu's land annually produced 2.4 million *koku* of rice.

Hideyoshi did not have the pedigree to become a shogun. He married a woman from an elite samurai family so that an heir would be eligible for the shogun position. The two issues that preoccupied Hideyoshi during the last decade of his life were his desire to bring China to submission and raising his only son, Hideyori. Some historians conclude that Hideyoshi's success in Japan turned him into an irrational megalomaniac. He wanted to make the world submit to him; he even sent armies to conquer Korea.

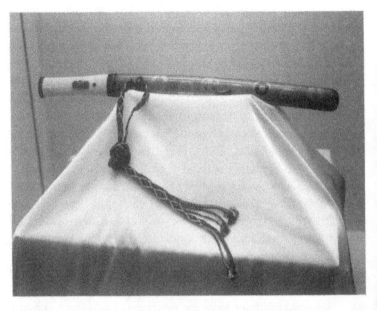

During the Tokugawa era, only samurai were allowed to carry the short sword.

The final years of Hideyoshi were difficult as he appeared to lose touch with reality. His armies on the Korean Peninsula suffered great losses and retreated in disgrace. He was also obsessed with protecting his son, Hideyori. On his deathbed his five top generals swore a blood oath that they would act as a regent for the young Hideyori until he grew into manhood.

Tokugawa Ieyasu (1542–1616)

Hideyoshi's generals swore allegiance to his heir, Hideyori. One of these leaders, Tokugawa Ieyasu, actually moved to the Osaka castle where Hideyori and his mother resided. It became obvious to the other commanders that Ieyasu was positioning himself to become Japan's next shogun. Consequently, the officers of Japan's western provinces allied against Ieyasu and the leaders of eastern Honshu. Ieyasu and his associates won the decisive battle, which took place on October 21, 1600, at a place called Sekigahara in Mino Province. For the moment, he allowed Hideyori to remain at Osaka.

Following this victory, Tokugawa Ieyasu made a dizzying set of changes throughout the land. In 1603 he accepted the title of shogun. To make sure that there would be no rivals after his death, Ieyasu marched against the Osaka castle. In 1615 Toyotomi Hideyori and his mother committed suicide when Ieyasu's forces stormed the Osaka castle.

A portrait of Tokugawa Ieyasu.

Tokugawa Japan (1600–1868)

Tokugawa Japan is one of the great paradoxes in human history. This period in Japanese history is also known as the Edo era because the Tokugawa castle was located in Edo. The seeming contradiction of this period is that for almost three hundred years Japan was under martial law though Japan did not have to fight a single civil or foreign war. Imagine having a country at peace for almost three hundred years! One need only count the various wars the United States has fought during its first two hundred years to realize how amazing it is to have almost three hundred years of peace.

The Tokugawa era was the foundation that modern Japan built upon. *Bakufu* policies that were implemented during the first decades of the seventeenth century guided Japan for the following two-and-one-half centuries. Brief descriptions of these key policies are noted in the following pages.

Daimyo and Division of the Land (Sankin Kotai)

Thanks to the detailed land surveys of the Hideyoshi period, Tokugawa Ieyasu knew how much taxable land was available for the *bakufu*. The problem was how to manage all of Japan's land. His solution was to divide Japan into various domains (*han*). In 1614 there were 192 *han*; this number grew to 262 by 1720. The size of the *han* varied widely. The Sendai *han*, for example, consisted of 1,018 villages while the Tannan *han* only had 23. However, the real measure of a *han's* importance

Edo Japan was divided into various domains. This is a nineteenth-century plate that indicates the domains' borders.

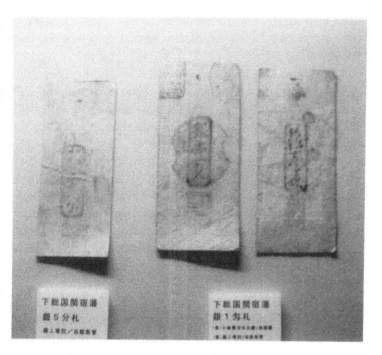

During the Edo era, daimyo started issuing paper money to be used in their particular han, *or domain. This was to supplement the growing deficit spending. This is paper money from one of the 244* han *that did this.*

was the amount of rice it produced. Every *han* had to produce at least 10,000 *koku* of rice. At the outset of Tokugawa Japan there were 26 *han* that annually produced at least 200,000 *koku* of rice. Most *han*, however, had an annual output of less than 50,000 *koku*.

Of paramount importance for the *bakufu*, however, was the establishment and maintenance of law and order throughout Japan. The Tokugawa policy was most brilliant in this regard. Ieyasu assigned individual daimyo (military governors) to maintain control over the *han*. The daimyo were categorized into three divisions. Daimyo of the immediate Tokugawa house received one-third of Japan's land. *Fudai* daimyo were those generals who were vassals of Ieyasu and supported his rise to shogun; they also received one-third of the land. Finally, in a diplomatically astute move, Ieyasu provided his enemies with land. These *tozama*, or outside daimyo, received close to one-third of Japan's territory. By equitably distributing this property, the *bakufu* did not alienate its allies or foes.

The shogun reserved the right to assign and move daimyo whenever and wherever he pleased. Indeed, between 1615 and 1650 ninety-five *han* were confiscated or restructured. During this same time period, 250 domains were transferred to various daimyo. As one author noted, "Never in the history of Japan had so much violence been done to local autonomy." Shoguns established their unquestioned authority early in the Edo period and backed up their dominance with intimidation. In 1634, for example, Iemitsu, the third Tokugawa shogun, visited

This is Doi Toshitsura, a nineteenth-century daimyo in typical dress. He is also known as the "snowflake daimyo" because of his study of snow crystals.

Kyoto and brought with him an army of 307,000—the largest mobilized force to date in Japan.

Daimyo operated within specified rules. Each daimyo had to establish a castle town on his domain. This served as the *han's* administrative center. These bases were crucial because the Tokugawa shoguns created a very schematized society. Accordingly, all samurai were ordered to pledge undying loyalty to a daimyo of their choice. This devotion was passed on to each generation and was reinforced as the samurai lived in the daimyo's castle town. In fact almost all samurai, who comprised 7 percent of the population, lived in the castle towns, which became booming urban centers. More details on Tokugawa Japan's population and growing urbanization are noted in subsequent sections.

If each daimyo enjoyed loyal samurai retainers, an economic base from his *han* peasants, and an impressive castle from which to rule, what would stop a semi-independent general from once again taking up arms against a weak or geographically distant shogun? Ieyasu understood the precarious nature of Japan's unity. Thus, the *bakufu* instituted a law wherein every daimyo had to build a second home. This second residence had to be located in Edo and was occupied by the daimyo's first wife and first son. Furthermore, the daimyo had to reside in his Edo home every other year. This policy was called *sankin kotai* or alternate attendance. In short, the shogun held every daimyo's family hostage in Edo. The future daimyo were raised at the *bakufu,* and this engendered loyalty to the Tokugawa house.

The Role of the Peasants

At the turn of the seventeenth century Japan had close to thirty million people, which was larger than any European state at the time. The ideology that unified Tokugawa society was Neo-Confucianism. One element of this worldview was the doctrine of strict social divisions. Society was divided, from most honored to least in this manner: samurai, farmers, artisans, and merchants.

Farmers made up 90 percent of the population and were the economic foundation of the state. As noted, the samurai lived in castle towns or other urban centers. Farmers provided the samurai a yearly stipend of rice, which meant that the warrior class did not have to work. Peasants also supplied the funds for the daimyo to build his homes, make semi-annual trips to the capital, support his family in Edo, and pay taxes.

Tokugawa Ieyasu noted that he wanted to make sure that the peasants "could neither live nor die." By providing the rural population with just enough food for sustenance, Ieyasu reasoned that there would be little time for peasants to scheme against political authority. Thus he consciously placed great economic burdens on the farmers. Surprisingly, it was this peasant policy that proved to be one of Ieyasu's few miscalculations. Against incredible odds, portions of the Tokugawa peasant class economically grew to the point that by the nineteenth century an identifiable rural middle class was more affluent than the samurai class. How did this happen, given the farmers' numerous financial constraints? The answer is multifaceted but is an instructive study on Japanese characteristics.

Farmers improved their situation by land-reclamation projects. During the first hundred years of Tokugawa rule, cultivated land increased by 82 percent. Since taxes were assessed at a flat rate, farmers had surplus funds from their annual yields. Peasants used these additional funds for research and development. Farming communities purchased and carefully studied books on fertilizers, various strains of rice, and soils. More sophisticated agricultural tools were also developed. With more arable land, better tools, and a greater understanding of fertilizer use, some *han* were able to produce more than enough rice for the daimyo, samurai, and annual taxes. Tokugawa peasants moved away from subsistence farming to commercial agriculture. Thus, sandy soil, often seen as useless because it could not produce rice, was now used to grow melons and other fruits. Cotton and raising silkworms were also major commercial endeavors. Surprisingly, rice was the most significant commercial crop. With their excess rice, Japanese farmers created breweries to manufacture rice wine (sake). Urban residents purchased these luxury goods, and business was so brisk that by 1750 more land was used for commercial agriculture than for subsistence farming.

A darker side of the economic growth in rural Japan was the self-imposed population control. Termed *mabiki*, or thinning, Japanese couples began the practice of infanticide. Unwanted babies were taken to the periphery of the village where they died of exposure or starvation. More effective farming tools meant that fewer hands were needed to plant and harvest. A home with one or two children was considered more likely to advance economically than one where six children had to be fed, clothed, and cared for.

The Emergence of the Japanese City

In 1575, twenty-five years before Tokugawa Ieyasu's victory at Sekigahara, a European described Japanese cities in these terms: "At this point I wish I were a skilled architect or had the gift of describing places well, because I sincerely assure you that of all the places and houses I have seen in Portugal, India, and Japan, there has been nothing to compare with this as regards to luxury, wealth, and cleanliness." Even before *han* castle towns appeared, Japan was moving toward a more urban society. In fact, between 1550 and 1700 Japan became the most urbanized country on the planet. At the turn of the eighteenth century Japan had five cities with more than 100,000 residents, while all of Europe had fourteen. Seven percent of Japan lived in the big cities while only 2 percent of Europeans did; and Edo was the world's largest city in 1700.

Evening Shower at Ohashi *is part of the* One Hundred Famous Views of Edo. *This work was from the hand of Utagawa Hiroshige (1797–1858).*

While castle towns contributed to the urban growth in Japan, when the Japanese spoke about cities they would invariably mention the three biggest ones: Kyoto, Osaka, and Edo. These three urban centers played a pivotal role in Tokugawa Japan and the country's subsequent modernization.

Kyoto was the oldest of Tokugawa's "big three" cities. It had been the imperial capital for more than five hundred years. Before 1600 it was Japan's only major city, housing 200,000 residents. By 1750 its population had grown to 400,000. During Tokugawa times it was known for its numerous Buddhist monasteries. It is estimated that there were seven to eight thousand Buddhist temples in Kyoto. Since the emperor lived in Kyoto, there also were numerous Shinto shrines. The cultural sophistication attracted the country's greatest artists. More than one hundred daimyo maintained mansions in the city, adding to their list of houses in Edo and on their *han*.

Kyoto also was the center of the silk industry. There were over one hundred merchants and agents who lived in Kyoto who dealt exclusively in silk. The city housed seven thousand looms that employed more than 100,000 people. Raw silk also was imported to Kyoto and was dyed and embroidered in a manner unparalleled in the rest of the country.

Osaka, the second of the three great cities, was an ancient Japanese village. In 1496 it was chosen as a center for the Honganji sect of Buddhism. The town became more prominent when Toyotomi Hideyoshi made Osaka his headquarters. By the first years of Tokugawa Japan, Osaka had surpassed Kyoto in population. Its location on the edge of Japan's Inland Sea made Osaka a convenient port for those traveling from east and west. Osaka became the central rice market for Japan, with warehouses dotting the city's landscape. By 1700 there were thirteen hundred rice brokers in Osaka. Merchant houses grew around this trade, and daimyo used these connections to transfer funds from Osaka to their relatives in Edo.

Shipbuilding also was an important industry in Osaka. More than two thousand ship carpenters were employed on the docks. It was, however, the metal refining plants that dominated industry in Osaka. Led by the Sumitomo family, there were seventeen refiners in Osaka that employed 10,000 people. Copper was refined in Osaka, sent to Nagasaki, then exported to China.

Edo was the youngest but fastest-growing of Japan's three great cities. By 1700 it was the world's largest city. Up until the end of the sixteenth century Edo was a small village. A *jito* family built a fortress in the town during the sixteenth century, and then Ieyasu was sent there by Hideyoshi. He decided to remain there after becoming shogun and built a large castle. More than three thousand barges were needed to bring the massive stones for the Tokugawa castle in Edo.

Edo's population exploded during the seventeenth century. More than three hundred thousand samurai lived in the city. Daimyo built large homes in the upscale portions of the urban center. The main businesses in Edo were part of the entertainment industry. The immense service sector of Edo's economy led to large portions of the city resembling the slums of industrialized London. With a population of over one million people, Edo was the entertainment center of Tokugawa Japan as well as the *bakufu* headquarters. It is best compared to a combination of modern-day Las Vegas and Washington D.C.

Actors became celebrities during Tokugawa times. This is the actor Nakamura Nakazo as depicted by Katsukawa Shunko (1743–1812).

Edo was the central location for entertainment in early modern Japan. This is a picture of women in Edo's pleasure quarters.

Foreign Relations

One aspect of early Tokugawa policy was the decision to severely curtail Japan's international contact. The antecedent of this isolation policy was that during the Nobunaga/Hideyoshi unification process, Christianity came under attack in Japan. Missionaries were expelled because the government feared that this foreign religion was infiltrating all aspects of Japanese society. By the onset of Tokugawa Japan there were an estimated three hundred thousand Japanese Christians. During the first decades of Tokugawa rule, anti-Christian laws accelerated Christian persecution. In 1637 a large band of Japanese Christians unlawfully assembled on the Shimabara peninsula. For three months shogunate forces attacked the Christians at Shimabara. More than 37,000 Japanese Christians and rebel farmers died in the siege for Shimabara and this marked the stamping out of this foreign faith during the Edo era. Following its victory at Shimabara, the *bakufu* expelled foreigners from Japan. The only European group allowed to stay on in Japan was a small contingent of Dutch traders. Deshima, a tiny manmade island built on Nagasaki Bay, was the only area where the Dutch merchants were allowed to reside throughout the Tokugawa shogunate.

During the first decades of Tokugawa rule, every Japanese family had to register at a local Buddhist temple. Any person suspected of Christian leanings was forced to take an oath against this faith. If they refused to recant their Christianity, they were executed. Altogether, the Catholic Church now recognizes more than three thousand Japanese martyrs who died for their faith.

The only Western presence in Edo Japan was the Dutch. This is a Japanese children's book in the Dutch language.

The banishment of Christianity from Japan coincided with the *bakufu's* imposition of strict trade regulations. Nagasaki was the only port on which Chinese and Dutch ships could call. No other foreign vessels were permitted to dock in Japanese waters. Japan embraced isolation. In 1715 the shogunate decreed that the annual number of Chinese trading ships to Nagasaki could not exceed thirty. As each decade of the 1700s passed, however, fewer and fewer Chinese trading ships arrived in Nagasaki—the only Japanese port they were permitted to visit. The annual number of Chinese merchant ships in Nagasaki slipped from thirty in 1720 to ten in 1791. Dutch trading was negligible; some years not a single Dutch ship entered the waters of Nagasaki Bay.

Japanese were forbidden to leave their country and overseas Japanese could not lawfully reenter their homeland. Since Japanese were not going to send ships to distant lands, building large ships was outlawed. In short, international contact came to a screeching halt in Edo Japan; the Japanese came to call the Tokugawa era *sakoku* (the closed country).

Nineteenth-Century Crises

Japan's accomplishments during the Edo era are truly remarkable. Increased wealth, the growth of literacy, domestic and international peace, and state unity are just a few of the characteristics of this period. Nonetheless, the *bakufu* faced serious problems by the beginning of the nineteenth century. Domestically, the two most threatening issues for the shogun were the economic chaos throughout the land and a growing loyalty among samurai to the imperial house.

Because of increased wealth in the rural areas, Japan's economic and social structures were somewhat skewed by 1800. Merchants, the lowest class in Confucian ideology, gained enormous power because the *bakufu* and the *han* were chronically in debt to them. The shogun and daimyo survived by deficit spending and borrowing against future tax receipts. Farmers also lived more luxuriously than in the past and expected better compensation for their energies. The *bakufu* simply could not keep pace with these demands.

Some of the shogun and *han* responses to the economic crisis included an outright canceling of all debts due to merchants, increased taxation, trimming the annual samurai stipends, and restructuring loans. Some loan restructuring bordered on the absurd, such as repaying debts on a two-hundred-and-fifty-year payment plan. In short, the daimyo and shogun were in a difficult position: samurai stipends had already been reduced so severely that many in this class were at poverty level; daimyo could not mistreat the merchants or the loans would stop flowing; finally, the farmers were the economic backbone of Tokugawa Japan, and rural uprisings were increasingly threatening the stability of Japan.

To make matters worse, bad weather for three consecutive years during the 1830s created a food shortage throughout Japan. *Bakufu* policies were ineffective in stemming the tide of hunger. A growing number of samurai responded to this economic chaos by transferring their allegiance from the shogun to the emperor. Kyoto became a haven for dissident samurai who believed that it was time for the emperor to once again take control of Japan.

Pressure from Outside

If Japan's only problems had been domestic ones, the *bakufu* might have had better success at holding the country together. But Japan's difficulties transcended its internal strife. Nineteenth-century technological, philosophical, and international changes made the world a very different place than it had been when Japan closed its doors in the early seventeenth century. The Industrial Revolution produced the world's first superpowers. England boasted an empire upon which the sun never set and most of Asia had been divided up among Western colonial powers. Even more threatening to Japan was the fact that Russia had extended its empire to the Pacific Ocean and was now encroaching upon Hokkaido.

The Japanese also witnessed increased shipping traffic in Asian waters. Whalers from the United States plied the Japanese shores and Russian ships attempted to dock at Japanese ports. The Japanese would have none of this. Ships were driven away and numerous foreign sailors who landed on Japanese soil were imprisoned, mistreated, and in some cases, executed. Still, by the middle of the nineteenth century Japan had fared much better than the rest of Asia. Unlike its surrounding neighbors, Japan's sovereignty had not been disturbed by Western industrialized states. Nonetheless, the

Nagasaki-based Dutch merchants knew that it was only a matter of time until Japan would be forced open by a western power. In an 1844 letter, William II of Holland wrote these words to the shogun: "The intercourse between the different nations of the earth is increasing with great rapidity. An irresistible power is drawing them together. Through the invention of steamships distances have become shorter. A nation preferring to remain in isolation at this time of increasing relationships could not avoid hostility with many others."

Japan remained immune from the imperialist powers, but by the mid-1800s two foreign countries generated concern among Japan's daimyo and the *bakufu*. Russian peasants and fur traders continued to move west until they reached the Pacific Ocean in 1638. During the course of the next two centuries, the Russians established themselves on the western rim of Siberia and ventured south to areas close enough to Japan to make the Japanese wary of an unfamiliar, encroaching neighbor. Russia's attempts to establish diplomatic relations with Japan were firmly rebuffed by the *bakufu*.

The second foreign country that had its eye on establishing diplomatic relations with Japan was the United States. The need for streetlights in America's cities provided employment for thousands of American whalers. Whale oil was the fuel that kept these lights burning, and sailors searched the oceans for these giant creatures. The migratory journey of some whale pods brought these behemoth mammals close to Japan's northern coast. American sailors who harvested whales off of Japan's coast often sought provisions from the Japanese, but were rebuffed and driven away. There were occasions when shipwrecked sailors were imprisoned for violating the *bakufu's* law against foreign intrusion on Japanese soil.

Asia also became more relevant to America as pioneers established vibrant communities on the Pacific coast. Only an ocean separated the United States and Asia. Furthermore, the gold rush of 1849 brought even greater prominence to the western portion of America. As the railroad tracks were laid across the United States, entrepreneurs longingly looked to the markets of Asia, and China in particular. Steamships replaced the windblown rigs, and it became clear that the United States desired a stake in the growing trade with China. Japan was a perfect stopping point for American ships to refuel and replenish supplies as they made their way to the Asian continent.

America and Japan

In 1832 President Andrew Jackson sent Captain Edmund Roberts to Asia with instructions to negotiate possible treaties with various Asian states, including Japan. Roberts was successful in procuring a treaty from Siam (Thailand), but he died before he could get to Japan. Even if he had lived, however, he probably would have met failure in Japan. In 1825 the *bakufu* reiterated its policy of isolation and demanded daimyo to drive away every foreign ship that dared to traverse Japan's waters. In 1846, the United States ordered James Biddle, its representative in China, to seek an audience with and, if possible, a treaty from Japan's leaders. When he arrived in Edo Bay with two ships, he was told that Japan only spoke to foreigners through the Dutch in Nagasaki. He was physically abused by a Japanese soldier, and he subsequently left Japan without exacting any type of revenge. This emboldened the Japanese and gave them a false sense of security.

At this point the reader might assume that the Japanese behaved with such hubris because they were unaware of advanced Western technology and learning. In fact, the Japanese had diligently sought knowledge about the world from every source that the *bakufu* permitted. Every year the shogun required the Dutch to prepare a report about the state of the world. This was translated into Japanese and presented to the shogun and his advisors. At times the Dutch captains traveled to Edo and delivered oral reports on global events. The power of what became known as "Dutch Studies" is seen in the 1774 Japanese translation of a Western book concerning human anatomy. This volume proved to be a catalyst for increased interest in Western science and technology. Medical personnel in Japan were astounded at the accuracy of the European study on anatomy compared with similar volumes from China or Japan. Eventually the *bakufu* withdrew the restriction against importing Western books—as long as they had nothing to say about Christianity.

Information about the West trickled into Japan. This limited knowledge created an insatiable interest on the part of students and teachers throughout nineteenth-century Tokugawa Japan. If familiarity breeds contempt, then rarity produces curiosity. "Dutch Studies" produced such a stir in early nineteenth-century Japan that Gampaku Sugita (1733–1817), one of the translators of the book on anatomy, wrote toward the end of his life that Western learning had grown in Japan like "a drop of oil, which, when cast upon a wide pond, disperses to cover its entire surface," a development that "brings me nothing but jubilation."

Not every Japanese shared Sugita's enthusiasm for the West. Japan was a military state and had been for three hundred years. A cornerstone of Tokugawa policy was the samurais' responsibility to defend the emperor and the land from intruders. Yet, there was a sense that the samurai class had grown lethargic and ineffective. One can hardly blame them. It is a bit paradoxical to have a nation under martial law for thirteen generations when there is no internal or external war. No matter, the samurai proved their mettle by repelling the initial Russian and American attempts to "open up" Japan. However, on July 2, 1853, Japan's world was abruptly shaken by the appearance of four uninvited ships from the United States.

Perry and the Opening of Japan

Unlike the rest of Asia and Africa, Japan had made it to the mid-1800s without succumbing to Western intrusion. Japan's geographical position, its limited natural resources, and the Dutch pessimism about potential commerce with the Japanese state contributed to the West's relative indifference to Japan. The shogun's noted rebuff of Russian and American inquiries about potential diplomatic ties kept the West at bay. However, America persisted and commissioned Commodore Matthew Perry to take a letter from the U.S. president to the emperor of

This painting's title provides all the historical context needed, "Perry Entering Yokohama Port."

Japan. Among other things, the letter indicated that America wanted Japan to sign a free-trade commercial treaty.

In 1852, when Perry left the U.S. East Coast for the long trip down the African coast up to the Indian Ocean and finally to the Pacific Ocean, the United States was stretching its borders. The western frontier now included the state of California, and America's land reached from the Atlantic to the Pacific Oceans. In the 1840s America's new national mission was to spread its ideal of freedom and democracy to all those capable of self-government. In fact, European Americans confiscated territories from native inhabitants in the name of Manifest Destiny—a phrase that characterized their belief that it was America's fate or fortune to spread freedom and civilization to places that lacked democratic institutions. The increase in the U.S. population, from 5 million in 1800 to 23 million in 1850, also encouraged migration to frontier areas, as land ownership became equated with wealth.

Thus, Perry was not only armed with several steamships— he also carried with him the American spirit of Manifest Destiny. His baggage also included every book he could find in the New York libraries—six altogether—on Japan. He wanted to be as prepared as possible when he entered Japanese territory. Japan's delay tactics, so successful in past encroachments, would not work on Perry, as he was aware that the Japanese had responded to past diplomatic requests by sending the missions to languish at Nagasaki.

The flotilla that accompanied Perry was meant to intimidate the Japanese. The U.S. warships were six times larger than

This rendition of Perry's officers is found in Tokyo's Koga Rekishi Hakubutsukan Museum.

any ship in Japan. There were sixty-one canons that jutted out of the ships' sides and a crew that numbered just under one thousand. There was a hint of gunboat diplomacy in Perry's actions. After delivering the letter to the authorities, Perry intimated that he would return in the spring and that there were fifty American ships in the Pacific that he could call upon for support. He retired to the China coast and received much-needed supplies.

Japan's Response to the West

Japan did not have a ministry of foreign affairs to assist in negotiating with the West. Instead, the *bakufu* response to American pressure was extraordinary—for the first time in Tokugawa history, it asked the advice of leading military governors and the emperor. The daimyo insisted that the shogun expel the Western diplomats. The shogun could not afford to follow this advice due to the West's military power. Perry returned in February 1854; Japan signed a noncommercial treaty with the United States on March 31, 1854. A decade later, Japan signed a series of treaties with the West that established relations between Japan and the industrialized countries.

The effects of the West's intrusion into Japan were immediate and filtered to all aspects of society. Edo Japan was not part of the international commerce and so its gold standard was lower than that of the outside world. After Japan signed the commercial treaties with Western powers, foreigners quickly bought up all of Japan's gold and sold it at a higher price on the world markets. The Japanese government responded to this plundering by recalling all its coins, re-minting them (with less gold in them), and then redistributing the monies. This caused inflation in the country, because people continued to receive their regular salaries but the money was not worth what it once was. Prices rose while wages remained at the same level.

For the 90 percent of Japan that farmed for a living, Western intrusion was both a blessing and a curse. It was a blessing in that there was a new market for cash crops. After Japan opened up to the West, numerous Japanese farming families transitioned from rice farming to growing cash crops, particularly products related to the textile industry. The curse was that the new economic system placed unsuspecting Japanese entrepreneur farmers at the whim of world market prices. By 1870, 90 percent of Japan's international trade was controlled by westerners living in Japan.

The unequal treaties that Japan signed with the West contained two onerous articles. First, the Western governments insisted that their citizens in Japan could not be tried under Japanese law. Termed as extraterritoriality, this clause insinuated that the West did not trust the Japanese judicial system. Finally, the West made the Japanese agree that Western countries would determine import tariffs. This placed Japan at a distinct economic disadvantage in its ability to be competitive domestically or internationally.

As each year passed, the Tokugawa house appeared weaker in its ability to stave off Western intrusion. Disgruntled samurai and daimyo threw their support behind the heretofore-symbolic leader of Japan, the Kyoto-based emperor. In 1867 Tosa, Mito, Chōshū, and Satsuma daimyo allied with each other against the Tokugawa house. Just one year later the Tokugawa government, which had been in place since 1603, was overthrown. The anti-government samurai were staunchly opposed to the concessions that its government had made to Western demands. The Japanese samurai theme was *Sonnō Jōi,* "Revere the Sovereign [Emperor], Expel the Barbarian." The disgruntled Japanese longed for a restoration of the imperial power. For more than a thousand years, the Japanese emperor lived in Kyoto and, for the most part, was merely a symbol that provided political and religious legitimacy in Japan. With the external pressure from the West, many in Japan believed that the answer was for the state to return to direct emperor rule. In fact, after the fall of the Tokugawa system, the emperor was moved from the ancient capital of Kyoto to Edo—renamed Tokyo (Eastern Capital).

This depicts the shogun's army fighting the imperial forces during the transition to the Meiji Era.

Meiji Japan
(1868–1912)

Quite paradoxically, the fall of the Tokugawa shogunate ushered in a period where Japan would embrace much of what the West had to offer. Emperor Mutsuhito (1852–1912), also known as the Meiji Emperor, was but a teenager in 1868 and so imperial advisors directed the affairs of the new government. Three months into the Meiji period (1868–1912), the emperor, as the mouthpiece of these advisors, published a five-point charter oath that established Japan's response to the West:

1. Deliberative councils shall be widely established and all matters decided by public discussion.

2. All classes, high and low, shall unite in vigorously carrying out the administration of affairs of state.

3. The common people, no less than the civil and military officials, shall each be allowed to pursue his own calling so that there may be no discontent.

4. Evil customs of the past shall be broken off and everything based upon the just laws of Nature.

5. Knowledge shall be sought throughout the world so as to strengthen the foundations of imperial rule.

The radical nature of this proclamation is difficult to fully comprehend in today's world. In it there are elements of democracy, a transformation of a completely schematized social structure, and a command to seek knowledge across oceans and continents.

In essence, the few advisors who surrounded the young emperor carried out a quiet coup against Japan's existing political and social paradigms. Three of these men were from Satsuma and Chōshū domains—the two areas that were staunchly anti-Tokugawa: Takamori Saigō (Satsuma), Ōkubo Toshimichi (Satsuma), and Itō Hirobumi (Chōshū). Prince Iwakura Tomomi, from the imperial house, joined the small ring of Meiji advisors. An astounding aspect of this leadership was that barely two years into governing Japan, three of these four leaders left Japan for a world tour to learn from the West. Leaving Saigō to direct the fledgling government, a fifty-person delegation left Japan in 1871, nicknamed the Iwakura Mission. Professor Marius Jansen writes about this expedition:

> Nothing distinguishes the Meiji period more than its
> disciplined search for models that would be applicable
> for a Japan in the process of rebuilding its institutions.
> Still, there are no precedents in world history for
> Japan's decision to send its government—fifty high

officials—accompanied by as many students and high-born tourists, to the Western world on a journey that kept them away from their jobs for a year and ten months from 1871 to 1873. That Japan did so is remarkable, and that the travelers returned to find their jobs waiting for them is more remarkable still.

Participants of the Iwakura trip visited twelve countries, and they took copious written and mental notes on their observations. Spending 205 days in the United States, 122 days in England, and 23 days in Prussia, the delegation had ample time to compare societies and watch governments in action.

Upon their return to Japan there was a more focused vision of becoming a modern, first-class nation. One encouraging observation that the Japanese travelers noted was the West's varied stages of economic and military might. Also, they recognized that the process of industrialization was a relatively recent development. Meiji's advisors preached patience. Still, Japan's goal was to build a *fukoku kyōhei*, "rich country and a strong army."

Japan's Modernization

Meiji leaders were convinced that Japan would have to make fundamental changes to become a modern state. Their travels abroad showed them that the Western nations' governments were much more centralized than Japan had ever been. In some sense, this was the easiest transition Japan would have to make, as the fall of the Tokugawa shogunate ushered in a government centered on one person, in one place. Shinto ideology was encouraged so that every Japanese person would realize that they were united in their obedience and devotion to the Meiji Emperor. The more than two hundred daimyo demonstrated their devotion to the emperor by donating their *han* to him. They were encouraged to do this by healthy buyouts. Within a generation Japan became one of the planet's most centralized states. But Japan's motive for centralization was nothing less than a desire to play in the big leagues of international relations. It was not so much that the Japanese officials were in love with the West; rather, they believed that by using Western technology they could one day stand up to Western chauvinism. Apart from increased centralization, a greater concern for the Meiji leaders was Japan's precarious economic situation. As professor Sydney Crawcour notes, "The major preoccupation of the Meiji government was to create a sound fiscal base for its needs." Indeed, Japan's drive toward centralization was an easier project than was the specter of transforming an economy that was not only bankrupt, but also not prepared for industrialization. Adding to Japan's economic problems was the Western powers' unwillingness to renegotiate the treaties that gave Westerners the power to determine the tariff on Japan's imports. It was difficult for the Meiji government to encourage small business startups when Japanese goods were undersold by cheaper imports.

One economic break that came Japan's way was a silk blight in Europe during the early Meiji years. Even before the

fall of the Tokugawa shogunate, Japan had doubled its production of raw silk between 1858 and 1863 due to the new
silk-reeling technology made available to local factories. The
government used the money from the silk exports to keep itself
afloat, but it was evident that drastic measures were needed to
make Meiji Japan economically viable. Western powers lined
up to offer loans to the Meiji advisors. Fortunately for Japan,
the Japanese spent some time in Egypt during their world tour
and observed Egypt's hardship due to foreign loans.

During their first years in power the Meiji advisors watched
as 30 percent of the government's revenues went to pay the
samurai stipends. Consequently, in a direct attack on the
samurai institution, the Meiji government ended these stipend
payments and in 1873 proclaimed the establishment of a con-
script army. Yamagata Aritomo, the father of Japan's modern
army, believed that the Prussian and French military systems
best suited the Japanese situation. In Japan every young male
was required to spend three years on active duty and four years
in the reserves. One can only imagine the betrayal that the
samurai felt at these machinations. They had fought to bring
about the Meiji Restoration and their victory resulted in their
greatest humiliation. They lost their identity and economic stability. For many samurai, including the Satsuma advisor Saigō,
this was too much. In 1877, the Satsuma samurai, led by
Takamori Saigō, rebelled and the government sent its new
army into battle. Saigō's defeat, and subsequent suicide,
marked the beginning of a Japan where every class was part of
the imperial armed forces.

Takamori Saigō was from the Satsuma domain. He was a prominent leader in the early years of Meiji Japan. He became disgruntled with the government's policies toward the samurai class and in 1877 he died while leading an unsuccessful rebellion against the government. This statue of Saigō is in Veno Park, Tokyo.

Japanese farmers also were treated to a new tax system that was based on Western patterns. Land tax was now assessed individually rather than at the village level. Taxes were fixed based on the government's assessment of land, and farmers paid their taxes in money rather than in rice. This was convenient for both the farmers and the government. The government was assured of a certain amount of annual land tax while the farmers prospered when market prices increased.

Meiji leaders were not content to have a country where everyone was fed and peace characterized the landscape. The goal was to be a first-class nation and the annual collected revenue was insufficient to move Japan to become an industrialized power. The government invested in infrastructure but it found that most of the state-owned enterprises were failures. Within this context, Meiji leaders implemented a policy that forever changed Japan's economy. Rather than expending energy on state-run industries, the government turned over entire sectors of the economy to private individuals. For example, when the government's shipping industry proved to be an economic fiasco, the government gave the Mitsubishi family its thirty ships and subcontracted the state's property to the private sector. This eventually produced the enormous *zaibatsu* corporations such as Mitsui, Mitsubishi, and Sumitomo.

One final drain on the new government's coffers was education. At the time of the Meiji Restoration it is estimated that 40 percent of all boys and 10 percent of all Japanese girls enjoyed some form of education. However, at least two of the five sentences of Meiji's Charter Oath addressed the issue of education: "Evil customs of the past shall be broken off and everything based upon the just laws of Nature; and knowledge shall be sought throughout the world so as to strengthen the foundations of imperial rule." After traveling around the world the Meiji elders proclaimed that Japan needed *bummei kaika* or civilization and enlightenment. This would be accomplished through Western learning. More than two thousand Japanese students were sent to Western universities while the government spent a substantial portion of its budget on more than five hundred Western professors who came to teach in Japan.

There are two aspects of Japan's education that should be mentioned. First, the government proclaimed to the Japanese people that there would be universal education. The Meiji advisors did not offer a plan to pay for this, they simply proclaimed that this was to take place, with the inference that the Japanese individuals, villages, and towns would be responsible to pay for it. Second, an emphasis in Japan's education system was on discipline and ingenuity. Two of the most popular books in early Meiji Japan were Daniel Defoe's *Robinson Crusoe* and Samuel Smile's *Self Help*. Both of these books were a testament to the "pull yourself up by your bootstraps" mentality. The entire nation was caught up in a frenzy to outwork its competitors and for Japan to take its proper place as a modern, first-class nation.

Education has always been a priority in modern Japan. This is a picture of Ōkuma Shigenobu (1838–1922), the founder of Tokyo's Waseda University.

This is a late-nineteenth-century view of Waseda University.

Meiji Constitution

The final factor that the Meiji leaders needed to make Japan a contender for great power status was a modern constitution where some type of representative government would mirror similar institutions of the world's most powerful nations. For the Meiji advisors, the delicate balance in this process was creating a semi-democratic state while retaining the bulk of power. Hirobumi Itō was largely responsible for the construction of the Meiji constitution. His overseas travels taught him one thing— Prussia was the power to imitate. Itō was so enamored with Otto Von Bismarck that he was accused of trying to emulate the physical movements of the Prussian leader, including the way he held his cigar! Using the Prussian constitution as a template the Meiji advisors created a government with an upper house of appointed statesmen, and a lower house of elected representatives. While less than 2 percent of Japan's population was eligible to vote, this still demonstrated to the world that Japan enjoyed a representative government.

A distinguishing mark of Japan's government versus the great powers of the day was the role of the Japanese emperor. The first chapter of Japan's constitution was devoted to the emperor, and it described the sovereign as sacred and inviolable; in other words, the emperor was divine and above reproach. In this way men like Itō continued to have paramount power in the government because they were the emperor's spokesmen. On January 1, 1889, the Meiji emperor presented the new constitution as his gift to the Japanese

Born in the year of the Meiji Restoration, Ozaki Kōyō (1868–1903) penned what is considered the Meiji era's most famous novel, Konjiki Yasha (The Golden Demon)*. A story about love, betrayal, and greed,* The Golden Demon *was made into a movie in 1953.*

people. England and then the other Western nations recognized Japan's new constitution as a modern or "Western" political institution. In 1894 Japan was finally able to revise the unequal treaties, removing the onerous extraterritoriality clauses (the Western autonomy on Japan's tariff laws was not changed until 1911). Moreover, while Western states applauded Japan's constitution, the document eventually became the instrument to justify future military incursions that brought on incalculable sorrows. It is instructive to note that one of General Douglas MacArthur's priorities as the Allied leader in post–World War II Japan was to create a new Japanese constitution that increased democracy while limiting the role of the imperial house.

Industrialization and Military Victories

Japan's society was thoroughly transformed due to Western influences. Its rigid social hierarchy was replaced by a doctrine that held that all human beings are born equal and every individual has the ability to rise above mediocrity—it just takes work! And work the Japanese did. Educators impressed on the Japanese children that the emperor deserved to have a country that was equal with all the other great nations of the world. Perhaps the greatest price that the Japanese paid to industrialize was the dehumanizing work that was required to keep factories running around the clock. Most of the labor in the textile factories was supplied by young women transplanted from the rural areas. Documentation proves that girls, sometimes as young as eleven years old, worked twelve to nineteen hours a day in cotton textile mills where the air was barely breathable. Their wages scarcely provided for their daily needs. Many of the young women whose health broke down in such conditions found that they could only survive by living off the streets and through prostitution. The *Hard Times* that Charles Dickens wrote about had found their way to the Japanese islands. Another example of the horrendous work conditions in Japan was the Mitsubishi-directed coalmines on an island that the Japanese termed "Battleship Island." This island, four miles from Nagasaki, had mines where people worked in temperatures that reached 130 degrees Fahrenheit. Men, women, and children shed their clothes as they descended into the mines—some of the tunnels were so low that miners could only work on their knees. There are documented stories of attempted escapes from the island; the unfortunate escapees were caught and killed. When cholera broke out on the island, the Mitsubishi supervisors burned the victims of the disease—some of the sick were burned alive. As Professor Carol Gluck of Columbia University notes, "Modern times are tough. . . . It is a very costly and miserable transition [to industrialization], and Japan did as badly and as well as the rest of these [industrialized] countries."

For Japan, the natural result of copying the West was to become a colonial power. Their incursions in neighboring Korea followed the pattern that they had learned from the West. In 1876, presenting an intimidating flotilla, the Japanese forced the Koreans to sign a treaty that gave Japan special privileges in three Korean ports, and also added the extraterritorial clause to the document. By 1885, 90 percent of Korea's exports went to Japan. Finally, in 1894 Japan went to war with China over the issue of Korea. Japan's victory over its much larger opponent granted it hegemony over Korea and Taiwan. China also paid an enormous indemnity that Japan used to further advance its push to industrialization. Ten years later Japan tested its mettle against imperial Russia and prevailed.

Its ability to stand up to a non-Asian state convinced the Japanese that they were now taking their place with the world's great powers.

Japan at the End of the Meiji Era

Japan accelerated its pace toward industrialization following its 1905 victory over Russia. Its victorious army in Manchuria, known as the Kwantung Army, remained on the Asian continent where it supported Japanese companies that were sinking their claws deeper into Manchuria's politics and industries. Korea, like Taiwan, became a Japanese colony. Japanese shipyards produced massive ships. Seventy percent of the needed iron ore for these vessels was imported to Japan from the Asian continent.

A defining moment for the Japanese occurred on July 30, 1912, when the Meiji Emperor died. It represented a passing of an era—a time of sacrifice, war, and rule by the oligarchy. Now Japan was poised to become a truly democratic society and was ready for social programs to take precedence over geographically distant military excursions. Not everyone wanted these changes. The showdown between Japan's competing ideologies is known as the Taishō Crisis.

Taishō Japan
(1912–1926)

During the Meiji era, the government was divided by the two houses in the diet, the elder statesmen, known as the *genrō,* and the lower house of representatives. While most power rested with the *genrō,* the lower house's influence was centered on the budget. Every year the upper and lower houses had to pass the national budget so that the government could continue to function. The *genrō* advocated a system that they termed a "Transcendental Government," inferring that the sacred and inviolable emperor was not subject to an elected body. National elections were irrelevant to the real source of power, the imperial throne. This ideology was endorsed by the *zaibatsu* corporations as they received major contracts from the government. The house of representatives saw things a bit differently. They believed that the people's voices ought to be heard through a democratic system. Unions supported this governmental paradigm.

The inevitable confrontation between these two ideologies occurred following the death of the Meiji emperor. The *genrō* could always point to their emperor for their legitimization. However, upon the passing of Meiji, his son, the Taishō Emperor, did not have the leadership qualities that his father possessed. In fact, Taishō was judged to be mentally unstable by those closest to him. With an aging oligarchy and a lack of a strong leader, the two houses of government had to work together more closely.

One reason that both houses tolerated each other was due to a surplus of funds with which to operate. Japan, in fact, enjoyed economic growth during the second decade of the twentieth century for various reasons. By developing their colonies, Japan profited from the cheap, if not free, labor from their colonial servants. Also, World War I presented a wonderful economic opportunity for Japan. Joining the French and British in this war, Japan occupied Germany's Asian colonies. It also stepped into the trading void in Southeast Asia as Europe, and then America, concentrated their resources on winning this drawn-out conflict.

One group that did not prosper during this period was the rural farmers. They could not compete with the price of the imported rice from Japan's colonies. Tokugawa farmers had maximized the arable land and so further land reclamation was not a viable option. Moreover, Japan's urban corporations ignored the rural population because of the farmers' limited economic power. Finally, it was difficult for the people in the countryside to supplement their income with local industries because of foreign imports.

The one institution that was concerned with Japan's rural population was the army. Farmers and soldiers believed that they were not receiving sufficient governmental attention. The military budget continued to decrease because the government used tax monies to improve Japan's social structure. At the same time, a larger portion of military recruits came from Japan's rural areas. Soldiers promised their poverty-stricken relatives that some day things would get better. In future years, when the radicals in the army sought support, they found strong allies in Japan's countryside.

Taishō Democracy

This period of Japanese history is referred to as Japan's experiment with democracy. Two major political parties, the *seiyūkai* and the *kenseikai*, gave Japanese voters alternatives at the voting booths, while the *genrō* or elder statesmen's power waned as many of them passed away. The bitter rivalry between the various political groups did not negate cooperation. From 1918 to 1921 Hara Kei assumed the post of prime minister. He was able to rally the various factions despite the enormous challenges he faced.

On the one hand, Japan reveled in its participatory victory in World War I. It had modernized to the point that it was considered one of the five great powers at the Versailles Peace Conference. In just a fifty-year period, from 1868 to 1918, Japan had astounded the world with its breathtaking speed toward modernization. On the other hand, however, the end of World War I brought with it the West's renewed interest in Asian markets and raw materials. Once again Japan faced keen economic

The entrance to the Yasukuni Shrine in Tokyo.

competition and tighter Asian markets as European colonial powers returned with a vengeance.

The Taishō era was also one of unprecedented social pressures. The Russian Revolution provided some rays of hope for disgruntled Japanese workers. Unions increased in size and influence. Prime Minister Hara Kei had to contend with strikes that grew in number and in effectiveness. Furthermore, Japanese from all walks of life, including women, were clamoring for voting rights. Until the 1920s, voting privilege was accorded to only about 2 percent of the nation's population.

Hara Kei was doing a remarkable job in juggling these social challenges, but was assassinated in 1921. For the next five years Japan tried to develop a path to democracy. Unfortunately, there were too many obstacles, and that path was diverted, leading the country into a cataclysmic war.

Tensions with the West

One main obstacle for the promotion of democracy in Japan was the growing disillusionment many Japanese had regarding the West. Western nations increasingly complained about Japan's growing empire and its influence in China. The hypocrisy behind these criticisms was too much for the Japanese to bear. Countries that boasted that the sun never set on their empires were critical of Japan's intervention in troubled neighboring states. The Japanese wondered how the British and the Americans could criticize Japan's actions in Asia when

Southeast Asian countries were ruled by geographically distant occidental states.

The Japanese believed that they needed to expand their territory because of Japan's limited arable space. Occidental countries established barriers to halt Japanese immigration into their territories. In fact, during the 1919 Versailles negotiations, Japan futilely attempted to insert a clause in the treaty covenant of the League of Nations that acknowledged equality between races. It believed that if this could be placed in the document, then Western governments could not discriminate in their immigration policies.

Japan was particularly disheartened by the manner in which the U.S. government treated Japanese immigrants. If America was supposedly the bastion of democracy, how was it that Japanese Americans were treated as second-class citizens?

The Japanese represented the second wave of Asian immigration to the United States. It was the Chinese who first came to the United States in large numbers. In 1850 China was in the midst of internal and external crises that forced many of its citizens to look overseas for relief. Hearing of mountains of gold in California, thousands of Chinese men left their families in search of riches. Less than 3 percent of the Chinese who came to America were women. Chinese men came alone, promising their wives and mothers that they would not be away from China for an extended period of time. Unfortunately, many of the Chinese men never made it back to their country and lived out a lonely existence in a strange land. Chinatowns represented the Chinese culture in American cities. Very few Chinese became fluent in English as the educational background of the

Chinese immigrants was quite low, and they remained on the periphery of white society.

In stark contrast, the Japanese who came to the United States did not intend to get rich quick and then return home. Because these travelers represented Japan, the Japanese government required potential immigrants to pass written exams. The Japanese who arrived on American soil were educated, culturally sophisticated, and eager to become part of America. They transformed the California swamps into luscious orchards. Despite laws that tried to keep Japanese children from attending public schools, Japanese parents encouraged their children to enroll in America's most prestigious universities.

Threatened by the Japanese Americans' success, some white citizens created physical as well as judicial barriers to keep this wave of Asian Americans from integrating into American society. A case in point is the passing of the 1924 Immigration Act. Anti-Japanese politicians, mostly from California, argued that anyone who was not eligible for natural citizenship should not be allowed in the United States. This legislation was specifically directed at the Japanese who were not eligible to become U.S. citizens. Arguing against Japanese immigration one congressman noted: "Of all races ineligible for citizenship, the Japanese are the least assimilable and the most dangerous to this country. . . . They come here specifically and professedly for the purpose of colonizing and establishing here permanently the proud Yamato race. They never cease being Japanese."

The Japanese ambassador to America warned that if this legislation, targeted against Japan, was approved, it would be difficult to maintain warm relations between the two countries. Some in Congress interpreted this statement as a veiled threat, which made them more determined than ever to pass the law. Japan responded by having a "Day of Humiliation" in Tokyo on July 1, 1924.

Japanese wanted their government to be an advocate for them against this blatant prejudice. If democracy was the best form of government, then why was it that elected officials could not defend the dignity of their citizens?

The Japanese government, however, had problems even larger than American racism to contend with. On September 1, 1923, at the noon hour when fires were being stoked to cook lunch, a cataclysmic earthquake hit the Tokyo/Yokohama region, the industrial center of Japan. Oil storage tanks cracked and the black liquid spilled into Yokohama Bay. Sixty percent of all Tokyo's structures were destroyed. Flames that were meant to cook the day's rice engulfed the entire region in a furious inferno. One hundred thousand people perished and many more were injured. In addition to the tragic loss of life, this disaster drained all of Japan's economic reserves. It took until 1928 for Japan to recover economically from the earthquake.

Social Revolution

During the Taishō democracy of the 1920s, Japan also under-went what one might call a social revolution. While the large industrial factories released workers, small businesses sprung up across Japan. Urban workers had access to newspapers and other printed material that condemned capitalist exploitation. The people's voices were rising to the fore of Japanese politics.

In rural Japan similar transformations were taking place. Though tenancy was the norm for farming families, the traditional hierarchical relationship between landowners and tenants was slowly changing. Rural folk may have been poor, but generally they were well-educated. Despite competition from their newly acquired colonies, Japanese farmers continued to push for social equity.

With such immediate foreign and domestic problems during the 1920s, one can understand how Japanese politicians may have missed the dark clouds looming on Japan's horizon—clouds portending a storm of such magnitude that Japan would be brought to the brink of annihilation.

Japan's imperial army and navy felt slighted by the Taishō democracy. Their simmering frustrations eventually boiled over. Friction between the government and the military had been brewing for years. In fact, at the very outset of the 1920s, members of the imperial navy believed that the government had betrayed them.

This story begins with the end of World War I. Declaring this to be the war to end all wars, architects of the peace agreements reasoned that if nations balanced each other in terms of armament buildup, then one nation would not rise to dominate the rest of the world. As such, the greatest navies in the world met in Washington in 1921 to place a quota on the number of battleships that each nation could build. Although other nations were represented at the conference, the three major naval powers at the time were the United States, Britain, and

Japan. A quota of 5:5:3 was agreed upon. That is, for every five capital ships and cruisers that the British built, the United States could construct five, while the Japanese could build only three. The rationale behind this arrangement was that Japan had only one ocean to patrol while Western nations had fleets in two or more oceans. The Japanese did not see it this way. One Japanese officer looking back on the signing of the treaty noted, "This was the day World War II began." Others in the imperial navy observed that this treaty said nothing about limitations on building cruisers, destroyers, or submarines, and that the treaty was only binding for fifteen years.

Of even greater concern to the Japanese military leaders was the continued decrease in military appropriations in the government's annual budget. The military was the primary casualty in Japan's growing democracy, which allowed for increased expenditures for social programs and the rebuilding projects of earthquake-devastated Tokyo. Every year generals and admirals had less money with which to operate. In 1922 the military received 42 percent of the national budget; by 1927 this had shrunk to 27 percent.

Manchuria was the one bright spot for the generals during the 1920s. It was also the bane of the civilian government's existence. Following its 1905 victory over Russia, Japan's army in Manchuria, known as the Kwantung Army, continued to occupy parts of northern Asia. The Russo-Japanese War cost so many lives that there was hardly a Japanese family that was not affected by the loss of a loved one. During the war, young Japanese soldiers' lives were sacrificed in taking key positions on Asia's mainland. Consequently, the public was emotionally invested in Manchuria and the government faced public resistance anytime it even suggested recalling the Kwantung Army.

For its part, the army insisted that the instability of the area necessitated its presence in Manchuria. Indeed, much had happened in China since the first Japanese soldier set foot in Manchuria. In 1912 China's two-thousand-year tradition of imperial rule came to an end. An experiment with democracy immediately following the fall of Pu-Yi, China's last emperor, ended in disaster. Dr. Sun Yat-sen, the architect of Chinese democracy, fled for his life as military warlords divided China into various spheres of influence. China's domestic chaos provided an opportunity for foreign governments to increase their influence there. Cities like Shanghai and Canton became playgrounds for foreigners in China. Numerically, however, the Japanese in China outnumbered the rest of the foreigners combined.

These developments led to an issue in Japan that became known as "The China Question." In short, the Japanese were appalled at what China had become. The once-magnificent empire that towered over the rest of Asia was now the butt of international jokes. The very phrase "to be shanghaied" had pejorative overtones. Japan was a self-professed enlightened Asian nation and many believed that it was the country's destiny and responsibility to spread this enlightenment to the rest of Asia in general, and to China in particular. The problem was that Asian countries did not want Japan's enlightenment. Korea and Taiwan already had fallen into Japan's expanding empire, and the exploitation that Korea endured under Japanese rule was known throughout the region. Thus, China believed that the benevolent rule that Japan wanted to establish over its neighbors was nothing more than a screen behind which was hidden their real desire to become a richer and more powerful nation. In fact, some Japanese junior army officers frankly stated that the sacred emperor deserved to rule the planet's richest and most powerful country. In their eyes, conquering China was a step toward this goal. The emergence of a new, stronger emperor provided these officers with the inspiration to pursue their aims in Manchuria. This was Manifest Destiny Japanese-style.

Shōwa Japan
(1926–1989)

The Rise of Militarism (1927–1936)

Christmas Day of 1926 brought with it sad tidings for the Japanese nation. On this day, the Taishō emperor's troubled life came to an end. During his reign his mental instability grew so severe that in 1921 his eldest son, Hirohito, assumed regency for his father. However, it was not until December 28, 1926, three days after his father's death, that Hirohito ascended to the throne.

Emperor Hirohito did not suffer from his father's ailments. He was well-educated—raised by military tutors—and he came to the throne having already traveled around the world. He quickly became the idol of his nation, especially the Japanese imperial army and navy. The military was in need of a strong leader because the China Question was becoming more complicated every day.

Of great concern to the Japanese military was the potential reunification of China. During 1926, China's Nationalist Party (the Kuomintang, or KMT) was headquartered in Canton, a key southern Chinese city. After years of preparation, the KMT began a methodical march north with the intention of removing warlords, uniting the country, and establishing democracy. Led by General Chiang Kai-shek, the KMT enjoyed marvelous success in what became known as the Northern Expedition. In just a matter of months Chiang Kai-shek had established his capital at Nanking.

At this time, Chang Tso-lin was the warlord in northeast China, which included the region of Manchuria. Through bribery, Japanese interests in the area grew under Chang's watch. However, the Kwantung generals were uneasy with the growing unity of China as this could result in the expulsion of Japanese troops from Manchuria. They were also frustrated by the warlord's seeming weakness in the face of the KMT's advancing armies. In a surprising move, Japanese military personnel in Manchuria planned and successfully executed the assassination of Chang Tso-lin on June 4, 1928.

This action demonstrated a disturbing trend in Japan's military system: junior officers were making major decisions without permission from their superiors. When Prime Minister Tanaka heard what the Kwantung officers had done he was quoted as saying: "What fools! They behave like children. They have no idea what the parent has to go through."

It became increasingly difficult to reprimand the army in Manchuria, because this was the one bright spot for Japan in the late 1920s. By 1929 Japan's economy had recovered from fiscal pressures that the 1923 earthquake caused. Just as Japan caught its economic breath, however, it faced a worldwide depression. On Thursday, October 24, 1929, the New York Stock Market crashed. The ripples of Black Thursday spread across the Pacific, crippling Japan's economy. Between 1929 and 1931 Japan's exports fell by half. One million urban workers lost their jobs and roamed the streets looking for any type of employment.

In the midst of this bleak situation, Japan was invited once again to participate in a naval conference. The purpose of this 1930 London-based meeting was to extend the ratio of ship-building beyond the 1921 level to include a more comprehensive list of naval vessels. Japan remained at what it considered to be a disadvantage with a continued 5:5:3 ratio on large cruisers. The shock and disappointment that the Japanese felt at the London Naval Conference manifested itself when an ultranationalist shot Prime Minister Hamaguchi in 1930; the prime minister subsequently died from his wound.

Frustration boiled over in Manchuria as leaders in the Kwantung Army believed that the Japanese politicians who preached international cooperation were compromising the country's well-being with empty promises of international peace. They also believed that democracy and cooperation with the Western powers were responsible for Japan's economic slump, the anti-Japanese legislation in white countries, and a second-rate navy. The Kwantung Army's response to these politicians was to make independent decisions and policies in Manchuria.

On September 18, 1931, Japanese soldiers detonated explosives on a railroad track and used this as a pretense to push out all Chinese troops from Manchuria. The Kwantung Army also took control of the political and social centers of Manchuria. Japan's paramount influence in the area caused the U.S. Secretary of State, Henry Stimson, to announce in January 1932 that the United States would not recognize territory that Japan forcefully incorporated into its empire. To add weight to the statement, President Hoover ordered portions of the U.S. fleet to move from the west coast to Pearl Harbor, Hawaii.

To lend legitimacy to its intrusion into Manchuria, Japan established the new independent state of Manchukuo on March 1, 1932. They brought in the previously noted last emperor of China, Pu-Yi, as the new political head of Manchukuo. China asked the League of Nations to inspect the area and to condemn Japan for its intrusion into Manchurian politics. Lord Lytton, the League of Nations' representative, traveled to the area and concluded that Manchukuo was nothing more than a puppet state of Japan.

Meeting at Geneva in October 1932, the League debated whether to recognize Manchukuo or to censor Japan for its actions. Matsuoka Yōsuke, who had spent much of his life in the United States and was multilingual, spoke on Japan's behalf. He noted that Japan was bringing stability to a region that had only known hardship for many generations. Despite his eloquence, Matsuoka was the only member of the League that voted against censoring Japan (Siam did not cast a vote while the remaining forty-two members condemned Japan). After the vote the Japanese delegation marched out of the building, and a few months later it withdrew from the organization. When Matsuoka returned to Japan he received a hero's welcome.

Meanwhile, there were still some Japanese who believed that their leaders were not moving the country into militarism quickly enough. On May 15, 1932, a group of young military officers broke into the prime minister's home and assassinated him. Though stability was quickly returned to the capital and the assassins were punished, it was clear that Japan faced a crisis. Now considered an international outlaw because of its actions in Manchuria, still mired in an economic depression, and under continued pressure from radical elements in the military, politicians suspended the party politics that had characterized the 1920s Japanese government. The government now was led by an inner cabinet comprised of five men. Moderates in the military were appointed to key positions in the cabinet so as to placate the more radical wing of the army. Between 1932 and 1945, eight of the eleven prime ministers were from the military. Governmental control shifted in favor of the military.

Between 1932 and 1936, there was also a curtailment of freedoms in Japan. A law against dangerous thought was put in place. This regulation made it illegal for anyone to publicly or privately disagree with the government's policies. Communist and socialist leaders were imprisoned for speaking out against the rise of militarism. In the schools and in the public sphere a doctrine known as *kokutai* became the mantra for society. This principle reiterated the view that the emperor was divine, and the people (his children), owed him the deepest devotion. Militarists promoted this teaching because they did everything in the name of their emperor.

The years 1935 and 1936 were important for Japan because they provided the last opportunity for the leaders to abandon their headlong foray into war. As word got out to other naval powers that Japan was preparing to abandon the provisions of previous treaties, Britain and the United States invited Japan to London to work out their differences. The quotas in place from the earlier treaties were scheduled to expire in 1936, and so the Western powers intended to extend the years of the agreement. They found a very different attitude among the Japanese delegation in the 1935 meetings. The 5:5:3 quota was discarded because Japan insisted on greater parity with the United States. When their proposals were rejected, the Japanese walked out of the conference and indicated that they would no longer abide by past treaties. Members of this delegation were greeted as heroes when they returned to Japan.

It was also during 1935 that more overt confrontations between military factions came to light. There was a growing schism in the military. The group that believed that Japan needed to be reflective and more cautious in its military ventures was known as the Control Faction. The more senior military leaders ascribed to this paradigm. On the other side, however, was the Imperial Way Faction. Led by junior officers, this group insisted that there was no time or need for reflection about expanding Japan's empire. As "sons of the emperor," the Imperial Way officers believed that it was their duty to provide their sovereign with the world's greatest empire.

What did ordinary Japanese citizens think about this division? They were given a chance to voice their opinions in 1935 when Imperial Way leader, Lieutenant Colonel Aizawa Saburō, assassinated General Nagata, a leader among the more conservative

Control Faction. Aizawa used the trial as a podium from which he castigated those in Japan who hindered the expansion of the emperor's rule. He belittled the advisors of Emperor Hirohito, who preached caution rather than expansion of the country's territory. Many individuals cut off a portion of their little finger—a traditional sign of support—placed it an envelope, and sent it to Aizawa.

Aizawa's performance during the trial emboldened other Imperial Way leaders. They acted on February 26, 1936. As falling snow greeted the cold Tokyo morning, members of the radical arm of

Western films remained in vogue even during the rise of militarism in Japan. This is a 1936 movie poster from the Shōwaka Theater.

the military sprung into action. In an attempted coup, soldiers marched to the house of the prime minister with the intention of shooting him. They mistook the prime minister's brother-in-law for him, and they shot the wrong man while the prime minister was hiding in his closet. This was only a small part of a widespread plot. Other soldiers were successful in assassinating the Lord of the Privy Seal (a close advisor to the emperor), a naval admiral, the director of the Military Education College, and the finance minister. Several former prime ministers also lost their lives that morning. Though the radicals were able to occupy key posts throughout Tokyo, the coup attempt failed. However, many of the leading moderates were removed, which allowed for the increased presence of Imperial Way generals in government. This group used its influence to take the boldest step yet—an invasion of China. It set in motion the century's second world war.

Japan at War (1937–1945)

Threatening clouds are often visible long before the rain begins to fall. With regard to Japan, we have observed the approaching storm; however, the rain began to fall on Japan, and the rest of the world, on July 7, 1937. Using a missing soldier as a pretext, Japanese troops marched across the Marco Polo Bridge into Chinese territory, to find their man. It was later revealed that he had slipped away to relieve himself in private. Japanese troops and equipment crossed the Marco Polo Bridge and began an assault on the main cities of northern China.

Chiang Kai-shek was still the leader of the Republic of China (ROC), whose capital was at Nanking. Just months prior to the Marco Polo Bridge incident, however, the Chinese Communist Party (CCP), which was led by Mao Zedong, agreed to work with Chiang Kai-shek's government. The CCP's stronghold was at Yenan in north-central China.

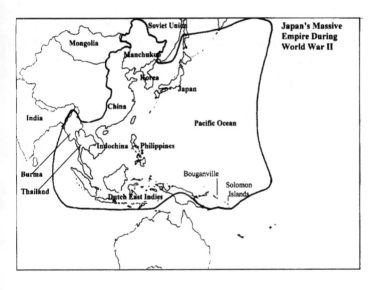

Japan's Massive
Empire During
World War II

Soviet Union

Mongolia

Manchukuo

Korea

Japan

China

India

Pacific Ocean

Indochina

Philippines

Burma

Thailand

Dutch East Indies

Bouganville

Solomon
Islands

In response to Japan's invasion, Chiang Kai-shek decided to try to stop the invaders at Shanghai. He believed that a battle for this city, which was home to thousands of westerners, would draw international attention. Despite his sending China's elite divisions to the coastal city, Shanghai fell to the Japanese. The Chinese army retreated several hundred miles west to Nanking. They were pursued by the Japanese army, which reached the capital in December of 1937. What followed has become known as the Rape of Nanking. Through the weeks of December and January, segments of the occupying Japanese force raped and murdered tens of thousands in Nanking.

Chiang Kai-shek's strategy was to retreat to China's vast interior in a classical "trade space for time" tactic. His army and government settled in Chongqing in Sichuan Province. The Japanese continued to conquer the eastern seaboard of China so that by the end of 1938 they controlled every major city and railway network in China.

When the emperor learned of Japan's aggression in China, he was told that China would surrender within six months of the initial invasion. However, several years passed and still Chiang Kai-shek's army held on. Outside aid from the British, Russians, and Americans helped the Chongqing government to survive. This foreign support inflamed the Japanese, who charged that the Western countries were not acting as neutral observers in the Sino-Japanese conflict. Then, in the midst of the deepening quagmire in China, the Japanese believed that they had received a gift from the gods akin to the *kamikaze* typhoon that destroyed the Mongols seven centuries earlier: on

September 1, 1939, Germany marched into Poland and Europe was plunged into war. Recalling the effects of World War I on Asia, the Japanese believed that the Western powers' preoccupation with their own countries would mean that Japan would have free rein in Asia.

Germany's occupation of France emboldened Japan to begin a steady move into French Indochina. This shift to the south was particularly attractive to the imperial navy. For years Japan's navy officers had jealously watched as their army counterparts gained victories on the Asian continent. Moving south meant that the navy would now be drawn into action as Japan sought to dominate the islands and the archipelagos of Southeast Asia.

France could not respond to Japan's incursion into Vietnam because France itself was occupied by Germany. However, the United States could respond to Japan's occupation of Vietnam, and did. On September 26, 1940, the United States imposed an embargo on scrap metal to Japan to demonstrate its disapproval of Japan's occupation of northern Vietnam. For its part, Japan responded the following day by signing a tripartite alliance with Germany and Italy. The treaty stipulated that each country pledged to come to the aid of the other should they be attacked by another party. At this time, the United States was the only major power not engaged in World War II. Thus, in both Japanese and American eyes, this treaty was directed against the United States.

Japan and the United States were heading toward conflict. Still, there were members of both governments who hoped to avoid a bloody confrontation. Japan's Ambassador Nomura Kichisaburō met with officials in Washington D.C. to try to reconcile the differences between the two countries. President Roosevelt noted that friendly relations between Japan and the United States could resume if Japan agreed to three terms: Japan must pull out of China, cease its southern expansion, and break its alliance with fascist Germany and Italy.

Talks between Japan and the United States hit a major barrier when in July 1941 the Japanese moved their forces into southern Vietnam. America immediately froze Japanese assets and placed an oil embargo on Japan. This was a crippling blow to Japan's war effort because 85 percent of Japan's oil was imported from the United States! A quick inventory showed that with its current oil reserves, Japan could continue its war efforts for only eighteen months. For many in Japan, the U.S. oil embargo was tantamount to a declaration of war. One Japanese official likened his country's position to a fish in a pond from which the water slowly was being drained.

At this point, Japanese leaders met with Emperor Hirohito and presented three options. The first was to acquiesce to U.S. demands and withdraw from China and Vietnam, which made a lot of economic sense. World War I proved that Japan could make economic gains while the rest of the world was at war. Yet, pulling out of China and Vietnam was not a viable option for the Japanese, as they represented an investment that Japan had made over the course of several decades. In 1941, 70 percent of the national budget was allocated to the military. Moreover, Japan envisioned creating a Greater East Asia Co-Prosperity Sphere. In this new world, Japan would lead the rest of Asia into economic and social prosperity, and all of Asia would be for Asians. To do this, Japan had to root out Western imperialism and replace it with a benevolent Japanese dominance.

A second alternative was to declare war immediately on the United States. The Imperial Way Faction advocated this route. Cooler heads prevailed and convinced the emperor that Japan needed some time to prepare if it was going to challenge America. Thus, the third option won the day: to negotiate with the United States but to prepare for war.

A casual observer might wonder why Japan would attack the United States—surely an assault wouldn't make America resume its shipments of oil to Japan. Planners of the imperial government believed that their country's future hinged on a continued steady supply of oil. The most convenient place to get this essential substance was in the Dutch East Indies, or modern-day Indonesia. Standing between Japan and the oil fields of Borneo was a north-south archipelago of seven thousand islands, known as the Philippines. In 1941 the Philippines was a colony of the United States. The Japanese knew that America would not allow Japanese ships access to the sea lanes they needed to get to this oil.

The summer of 1941 passed with no break in the U.S.-Japanese diplomatic stalemate. On September 6, 1941, an imperial conference was held where the militarists explained their plans of war to the emperor. According to one account, Emperor Hirohito was so frustrated with the militarists that his eyeglasses fogged up as he noted, "You said that it would take only six months to defeat China. It has been four years and still China is not defeated. Now you say you can defeat the U.S.

in three months—a country vastly more powerful than China." Nonetheless, military advisors persistently reminded the emperor that the United States was the aggressor as it had frozen Japanese assets and had mercilessly shut off Japan's primary oil supply. A compromise was arrived at as the meeting came to a close. The military would wait until the end of October before taking any action against America. In short, they would give the diplomats a narrow window of opportunity to repair U.S.-Japanese relations. In return for this delay, the emperor appointed General Hideki Tojo, a leader among the more aggressive militarists, to the position of prime minister.

Over the next few weeks diplomatic efforts yielded no results. The two countries were at an impasse, and plans were put in motion by the Japanese to turn their cold war into a bloody struggle for survival.

Japanese militarists, particularly the naval leaders, were convinced that they could not win a protracted war with the United States. Surprisingly, Isoroku Yamamoto, the architect of Japan's attack on the American installations at Pearl Harbor, was extremely pessimistic about his country's chances against America. Yamamoto spent some time in the United States and had studied at Harvard University. He was astounded by America's industrial potential. In his assessment of America, he noted that it was a sleeping giant. Yamamoto believed that Japan's only hope against the United States was to lead a surprise attack on its Pacific fleet at Pearl Harbor. He reasoned that the United States would respond by declaring war on Japan, Germany, and Italy. Initially, the United States would focus on the European theater. France was already occupied by Germany and England was in a desperate situation. Yamamoto correctly gauged that the war in Europe would continue for four years. If Germany won the war, then America would have to accept Japan's terms for surrender. If Germany lost, it would still give Japan four years to consolidate its Pacific empire so that the United States would seek a peace treaty rather than take on Japan's creation of the Greater East Asia Co-Prosperity Sphere.

Once Yamamoto's plan was accepted, debate raged about how to declare war on the United States. Diplomats insisted that Japan provide the United States with a formal declaration before it began dropping bombs on U.S. ships. Finally, it was agreed that the Japanese diplomats would give the U.S. Secretary of State official notice of impending hostility twenty minutes before Japan's planes would arrive at Pearl Harbor on December 7, 1941. Unfortunately, the message sent from Tokyo to Washington D.C. was not translated and typed in a timely fashion so that by the time the United States received official notice of Japan's intentions, the bombing of Pearl Harbor had already begun.

Paradoxically, the attack on Pearl Harbor represented both tremendous success and failure for Japan. It was successful in its mission of secrecy. Led by Chuichi Nagumo, the imperial fleet left Japan's northern Kuril island chain on November 26th. Nagumo's most difficult task was to stealthily take the large fleet across the Pacific. If the United States caught sight of the fleet or heard any radio transmissions, then the element of surprise would be lost. In a scene replayed in many Japanese patriotic movies, Nagumo brought his fleet across the planet's largest ocean undetected.

The Japanese navy surprised even itself in its minimal losses. While the United States had eight battleships that were either destroyed or damaged, and almost four thousand dead, the Japanese losses were relatively light: twenty-five planes destroyed and twenty-three dead. This certainly contrasted with Yamamoto's expectation that Japan would lose up to one-third of the ships sent across the ocean.

In the long term, however, Pearl Harbor represented a major loss for Japan. Yamamoto's main objective at the Hawaii naval station was to sink the U.S. Pacific fleet aircraft carriers. By doing this, Japan could roam the Pacific Ocean unchallenged. On December 7, 1941, not one U.S. aircraft carrier was at Pearl Harbor.

Furthermore, Nagumo did not send a third wave of attack planes on December 7 because of the first planes' dramatic successes. The mission of the aborted third wave was to destroy U.S. oil reserves on the islands. If Japan had done this, it would have severely delayed the American response to this attack.

Finally, Japan miscalculated the U.S. response to the attack. Rather than withdrawing and remaining isolated, Americans united in their resolve to stamp out fascism in Europe and punish Japan for its aggression.

In Asia, Japan unleashed its military might against the Western colonial states. Malaya, Singapore, the Philippines, Burma, and the Dutch East Indies were attacked and occupied after Pearl Harbor. Japan was no longer diplomatically restrained in its aggression throughout Asia.

Japanese citizens were informed of the military victories through a biased and misinformed press. Because of false reports, many Japanese assumed that the United States was on the verge of collapse and that Southeast Asians were welcoming Japanese troops with open arms. In fact, the Japanese had to fight tooth and nail to occupy Southeast Asian peninsulas, islands, and archipelagos. As for the United States, Japan learned that American military strength was alive and well on April 18, 1942. On this date, B25 planes from the U.S. carrier Hornet dropped bombs on Tokyo. While the actual damage caused by this sortie was minimal, it reminded the Japanese command that it remained vulnerable to planes launched from floating runways. Psychologically, it was devastating for the Japanese to see the vulnerability of their sacred land.

Responding to the B25 bombing, Yamamoto asserted that Japan had to take an even greater gamble than Pearl Harbor. The Japanese naval hero once again proposed to cross the Pacific. This time he himself would lead the attack with a fleet much larger than the one that was used at Pearl Harbor. The ships in this second trek across the Pacific, or what Ferdinand Magellan called the peaceful ocean, would include seven aircraft carriers, seven battleships, including his flagship, the *Yamato*—the world's largest battleship—forty-three destroyers, and thirteen submarines. The plan was for the fleet to sail north. At the Aleutian Island chain, Nagumo would take half of the ships and sail south to attack the U.S.-held island of

Midway. U.S. personnel at Midway would presumably radio for help, and the U.S. Pacific aircraft carriers would respond. As these U.S. floating machines made their way to Midway, Yamamoto would bring down the second half of the imperial fleet and the U.S. ships would be caught between Nagumo and Yamamoto's ships. If all went according to plan, the United States would lose its Pacific carriers, which would make America vulnerable to further Japanese attacks, if not invasion. It was a brilliant plan that led to one of history's greatest naval debacles. It was the turning point of the war, and perhaps the twentieth century.

Japan's navy lost the Battle of Midway because American ships were lying in wait for the imperial ships. American intelligence personnel deciphered Japan's secret code weeks before the June 4–6, 1942, battle. Thus, American pilots from their nearby carrier bases were patrolling the waters around Midway. They caught the Japanese navy by surprise and sank four carriers. An even greater loss for Japan was that it lost 3,500 men among whom were Japan's finest fighter pilots.

After the defeat at Midway, Japan turned its attention to defense rather than offense. In the Solomon Islands, Japan's advance was stopped and an effective counteroffensive by the Allied troops made Japanese generals pull back. To bolster troop morale, Yamamoto traveled south, but U.S. planes shot down Yamamoto's aircraft as it neared the island of Bouganville, and all aboard died in the crash.

Japan's dream of a Greater East Asia Co-Prosperity Sphere turned into a nightmare. Initially, some nationalistic Southeast Asian leaders welcomed the Japanese because they believed that the Japanese would expel Western colonial powers. What Southeast Asians did not count on was that their East Asian neighbor would prove to be a harsher colonial power than the Western countries. The Japanese sense of cultural and ethnic superiority manifested itself in their mistreatment and belittlement of other Asians.

Despite Japan's early successes, it proved impossible to translate these victories into economic stability. Japan was stuck in a land war in China, while its navy patrolled the planet's largest ocean. It simply was not feasible for Japan to produce

This is a November 1942 movie poster. The writing on the side reads, "We will keep winning a second year." This is a reference to the Pacific War, not the movie.

enough material to sustain its military operations. At the same time, the United States demonstrated immense power by providing more military material than the rest of the world. Thus, while Japan strained to maintain its armies, the United States was just starting to reach its potential as the world's new superpower.

Bloody battles occurred between American and Japanese soldiers for strategic Pacific islands and atolls. For example, the Japanese furiously clung to Saipan, in the Northern Mariana Islands. One chronicler estimates that of the 32,000 Japanese on

A woman in the ruins of Tokyo during World War II.

Saipan, only 1,000 survived following the July 1944 battle against the U.S. forces.

Once Saipan fell, U.S. bomber planes used the island's runways to launch their raids against Japan. Beginning in the fall of 1944, U.S. pilots began regular bombing sorties against Japanese munitions factories and key aspects of Japan's industrialized infrastructure. Beginning in March 1945, however, U.S. pilots began bombing residential areas of Japan's cities. In the first night of such bombing 84,000 Japanese perished.

On April 1, 1945, U.S. troops landed on Okinawa—an island south of Kyushu. More than 100,000 Japanese soldiers were well-positioned in the mountains that overlooked Okinawa's shores. Despite their heroic stand, the emperor's soldiers could not drive off the invaders. During the Battle of Okinawa, Japan's desperate situation was evidenced as teenaged boys climbed into planes on suicide missions. Yet, of the 355 kamikaze pilots that made this final flight, only 60 were able to reach their targets, and the suicide missions destroyed only six U.S. vessels off Okinawa. The Japanese navy had only enough fuel for the massive *Yamato* battleship to make a one-way journey to the nearby island of Okinawa. Even before the *Yamato* could reach the fight, it was spotted by U.S. pilots, who easily sank the pride of Japan's navy. More than 2,500 personnel drowned as the ship broke apart.

Just days following the U.S. assault on Okinawa, Germany surrendered, which allowed the Allied forces to concentrate on their Pacific campaigns. On June 21st, the Japanese forces on Okinawa surrendered, leaving American troops at Japan's doorstep. One month later the Allied leaders met at Potsdam,

Japanese pilots used these planes, also known as Japanese Zeros, to attack portions of Southeast Asia.

Germany to discuss, among other things, the strategy for victory against Japan. President Harry Truman insinuated that the United States had a weapon of mass destruction that would shock the world.

Since the beginning of the war, the United States had heavily invested in creating an atomic bomb. Nicknamed the Manhattan Project, American scientists created individual bombs that were capable of wiping out entire cities. After successful tests of the atom bomb, President Truman authorized the transport of the weapon to the island of Tinian in the Marianas chain. The USS *Indianapolis* delivered the bomb, nicknamed the "Little Boy," to the American forces on Tinian and then headed toward the Philippines. While the USS *Indianapolis* completed a successful journey to deliver the bomb, the ship was torpedoed as it steamed toward the Philippines. Of the 1196 men on board, only 316 survived the initial blast and the subsequent days in the sea. The ship, because of its secret mission, was not listed as missing until several days after it was sunk, and so the survivors languished in the sea for more than four days until they were spotted from the air by an American pilot.

With the bomb in place, the Allied leaders presented Japan with an ultimatum from Potsdam: surrender unconditionally or suffer unparalleled destruction. Japan refused to surrender, and so President Truman authorized the use of the atom bomb. The target chosen was Hiroshima, as it had not been devastated by earlier bombings. On August 6, 1945, the world was introduced to atomic warfare. One bomb leveled Hiroshima and

200,000 people perished, some from the initial blast and others from later radiation sickness.

Two days later, Russia declared war on Japan. The Japanese Kwantung Army in Manchuria was taken by surprise as Russian tanks and heavy artillery flowed into northeast China. Japanese officials were particularly disheartened by this event because they hoped to negotiate with the Allied forces through Russian diplomats. Now Japan faced a new threat, and was vulnerable to attack from the north.

Reeling from these two developments, Emperor Hirohito met with his officials on August 9th to consider Japan's options. On that very day the United States dropped a second atom bomb on Japan. This time the target was the port town of Nagasaki. Even though this second bomb was more powerful, its destructive powers were somewhat curtailed because it was not dropped in the center of town. Nonetheless, the massive explosion destroyed much of the city and took the lives of tens of thousands. This second bomb encouraged the imperial house to request the imperial armed forces to surrender to the Allied armies.

When Emperor Hirohito informed his nation that it had lost the war he stated, "We must bear the unbearable." Japan was a nation with an impeccable record of military victories until World War II. It had defeated the Mongol hordes, China, Korea, Russia, and it was at the Versailles victory table following World War I. One cannot blame the Japanese for feeling invincible, given Japan's past combat record. Consequently, the Japanese had invested a tremendous amount of economic, mental, physical, and spiritual capital in their quest for victory over China and the United States. Its soldiers preferred death to defeat or capture. For eight years, Japan's energies were directed toward war and victory. Now, after enduring humiliating defeats and massive destruction from U.S. bombs, the Japanese found themselves at the mercy of the Allied victors.

Since the Meiji era, Japan's goal was to be a first-class nation—to be on the same playing field with the world's greatest powers. To accomplish this, generations of Japanese sacrificed their lives for the good of the nation and for the honor of their emperor. Thus, Japan's loss in World War II represented a moral, physical, mental, and spiritual defeat. Everything they had worked for and believed in appeared to be a lie. Their emperor announced that he was not divine, Japanese soldiers returned home with tales of humiliating defeat, and Japan's cities and infrastructure were thoroughly ruined by Allied bombing. Geographically, Japan's once-great empire was stripped away. Japanese overseas were sent back to their homes in the fall of 1945, and the population ballooned to 80 million up from the prewar number of 71 million. Another postwar shock to the Japanese was the discovery that they were despised throughout most of the world, particularly in Asia. Japan's string of victories came to an abrupt end and with it the Japanese assumption of superiority.

Given this postwar context, it is surprising—if not amazing— that Japan became the world's second leading economic power during the second half of the twentieth century. Its economic growth came about because of the people's resilience, external support, and international crises.

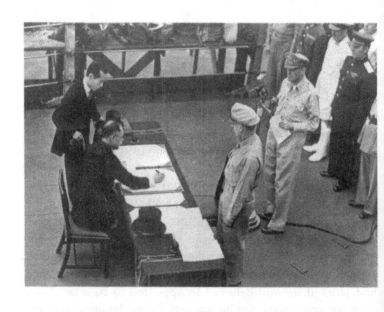

and with it not behind to sup . . . ne to be the

prove has . . . .ed for he second from Japanese

ished home . . . .ates of hostilities (clear and

Two views of the Japanese signing surrender documents on the USS Missouri.

The MacArthur/Yoshida Years (1945–1951)

Following Japan's surrender, Allied troops, primarily American soldiers, occupied Japan. Between 1945 and 1951, when the peace treaty was signed, American personnel assisted Japan in its recovery. General Douglas MacArthur was the Supreme Commander, Allied Powers (SCAP) in Japan. SCAP came to represent the headquarters where policies were discussed, proposed, and carried out.

The immediate crisis Japan faced was lack of food. With its colonies gone, Japan had to feed itself but its farmers could not produce sufficient grain for the nation. Urban people only survived by trading on the black market or living what they termed, "an onion existence"—trading away everything they had for food. MacArthur cabled his superiors in Washington D.C. to: "Send me food or send me bullets." The crisis was not solved overnight, but American soldiers distributed food and sold goods to the Japanese via the black market.

Of major concern to the Japanese was the future status of the imperial family. Many of Japan's enemies wanted to depose Emperor Hirohito and place him on trial. MacArthur believed that it was more advantageous to keep the imperial institution. He met with the emperor, and they had their photograph taken together. The picture was a shocking story of contrast—one that the emperor's aides tried unsuccessfully to keep out of the public eye. In the photo, the American general towers over the stiff, nervous-looking emperor. Even more shocking is the fact that MacArthur is not wearing a necktie while the Shōwa

USS Missouri *officers and a Japanese delegation examine Tokyo Bay mine locations following Japan's surrender.*

Emperor is very formally dressed. This image was on the cover of Japanese newspapers, and it was interpreted in various ways. Some saw it as the height of Japan's humiliation, while others viewed it as a symbol that MacArthur intended to support the emperor—he would stand by him. This, in fact, was the case, as Emperor Hirohito was not put on trial and was allowed to carry on as Japan's emperor.

Japan's political cooperation with the occupying force centered on Yoshida Shigeru (1878–1967). Though he was often accused of not possessing the political savvy needed to lubricate Japan's intransigent political machinery, Yoshida was the leader Japan needed immediately after the war. Between 1946 and 1954, Yoshida formed five of Japan's seven cabinets and served as prime minister for most of those years. He was fond of saying that it was possible that though Japan lost the war, it could win the peace. He worked with SCAP and the native political establishment to fulfill this prophecy.

While Yoshida and SCAP accomplished a great deal in the seven years following the war, there are three achievements that stand out: the 1947 constitution, the redistribution of farmland, and the restructuring of the economic system.

SCAP believed that the 1889 Meiji Constitution was responsible for the growth of Japanese militarism. Since that document began with the statement that the emperor was sacred and inviolable, it was used by the militarists and the emperor's advisors as a pretext for expanding Japan's borders. They reasoned that if the emperor is indeed divine and never wrong, then he deserves the world's greatest empire. MacArthur instructed twenty-five SCAP advisors that they had ten days to come up with a new constitution. Led by General Courtney Whitney, the group produced a document that not only transformed Japan but also has endured into the twenty-first century.

The role of the emperor was changed from sacred and inviolable to a symbol of the state and the unity of the people. He was to remain outside of the government. The document thus focused on issues unrelated to the imperial house, namely the need for Japan to nurture democracy, human rights, and peace.

The new constitution demolished the Genrō (Upper) House. No longer would non-elected oligarchs and aristocrats lead Japan. Furthermore, Japanese over twenty years of age, both men and women, were eligible to vote. Human rights were prioritized in the 1947 constitution. Women were not only given the right to vote, they were also given the right to divorce their husbands, to marry and divorce without their parents' consent, and to have legal abortions. Forced prostitution was outlawed so that daughters could no longer be sold into virtual slavery at urban brothels. Over forty articles in the constitution deal with human rights.

One fascinating and somewhat controversial aspect to the constitution is Article 9; also known as the renunciation of war article, it states that: "Aspiring sincerely to an international peace based on justice and order, the Japanese people forever renounce war as a sovereign right of the nation and the threat or use of force as means of settling international disputes. In order to accomplish the aim of the preceding paragraph, land, sea, and air forces, as well as other war potential, will never be maintained. The right of belligerency of the state will not be recognized."

Japan's postwar constitution limits the military budget expenditure. These tanks represent Japan's modern self-defense weaponry.

Given Japan's past, with the prominent role of the military, whether by shoguns, samurai, or generals, this article appeared to be wishful thinking. However, it is difficult to find a more peaceful country on the planet than Japan since the end of World War II. It has not engaged in any conflict, despite its proximity to countries in turmoil. The constitution also notes that not more than 1 percent of the nation's Gross National Product can be used for the nation's defense forces. Japan has not needed a large defense force because America has bases on the islands and has pledged to defend Japan. To put this in perspective, one can imagine how strong America's economy and society would be if another country were responsible for its defense.

When Japanese politicians were presented with this constitution they were shocked and disappointed. They wanted the emperor and his advisors to have greater power. Some officials were too ashamed to present the document to Hirohito. Nonetheless, the SCAP advisors told the officials that if this constitution was not accepted, it was possible that the emperor would be put on trial. This veiled threat pushed the Japanese politicians and the emperor to accept the document.

At the end of World War II 90 percent of Japan's farmland was owned by about 30 percent of the rural population. In short, most agrarian workers were tenant farmers. As tenancy rates were steep, very few Japanese farmers ever were in a position to own land. SCAP rectified this situation by abolishing the legitimacy of absentee landlords. If you owned farmland, you were required to live on it. Furthermore, the constitution mandated that the maximum size for farms was ten acres. Absentee landlords and people with large farms were forced to sell their land to the government. SCAP turned around and sold the land to tenant farmers, providing them with generous loan terms. The agrarian social engineering that these laws accomplished is something rarely seen in non-Communist countries.

Finally, the occupiers believed that the large *zaibatsu* corporations had to be demolished. These corporations profited from the war effort, and their inordinate hold on economic wealth overpowered smaller companies. SCAP went after more than three hundred family-owned businesses, including the Mitsubishi and Mitsui corporations. The success of this program was mixed. The large conglomerates were broken into smaller pieces, but many of the new companies went to allies of the families.

The democratic, human rights, and anti-large business sentiments of the occupying forces played well to those Japanese who had been oppressed for years. Socialist and Communist leaders who had been locked up in prison were released and welcomed to participate in Japan's new society. Unions grew in membership and were effective in stemming exploitation by big businesses. Small entrepreneurs enjoyed greater access into the economy while Japan's farmers owned the land they tilled. These social and economic changes were halted at the end of the 1940s because of political changes in East Asia.

Following the end of World War II, the truce in China between Chiang Kai-shek's Nationalist Party (KMT) and Mao

Zedong's Chinese Communist Party (CCP) ended. The Chinese Communists were very active in developing positive social change during Japan's occupation of China. In the KMT-CCP Civil War, the Communists received popular support and Chiang Kai-Shek ignominiously retreated to the island of Taiwan. On October 1, 1949, Mao Zedong declared the founding of the People's Republic of China, which meant, among other things, that the United States now faced two large Communist foes, the Soviet Union and China. In June 1950 Communist North Korea invaded South Korea, and the peninsula became the political and military chessboard of the world's great powers. These developments, along with the growing intensity of the Cold War, shifted certain U.S. policies in Japan. Both SCAP and the Japanese government backed away from their support of unions and organizations with any leftist leanings. The Korean War provided Japanese companies with opportunities to manufacture and sell a myriad of goods, and the *zaibatsus* were permitted to reassemble. In short, the United States needed a strong ally in Asia to offset China's move to Communism. American companies and the U.S. Congress insisted that Japanese entrepreneurs and corporations receive research and development assistance.

By the beginning of the 1950s, Japan had caught its breath. In 1951 it signed a peace treaty with the United States. Douglas MacArthur, so revered by the Japanese, was ignominiously fired by President Truman because, against direct orders, he provoked Communist China into joining the war in Korea. The Japanese knew they could move forward without outside guidance.

Japan's Economic Marvel

Beginning in 1955 and lasting for several decades, Japan's economy increased at an annual rate of 10 percent (above inflation numbers). This unprecedented growth placed Japan second only to the United States as the world's most powerful economic state. Several issues must be considered in understanding this spectacular growth.

Japan had an economy that was minimally tapped for defense funds. Furthermore, the American government made sure that research and development funds made it to Japan. It also must be remembered that Japan was the first Asian industrialized nation, and World War II did not change that. Southeast and East Asian countries did not have the funds, expertise, or infrastructure to develop quickly after World War II, and so Japan stepped into the gap. It is true that Japan had to rebuild most of its industrial plants immediately after World War II, but this was another blessing in disguise. Getting rid of the old and outdated machinery, Japan used the latest technology to redevelop its industrial base. In just a few years, Japan became the world's leader in building large ships.

An important boost for Japan was the creation in 1949 of the Ministry of International Trade and Industry (MITI). This governmental organization directed companies to develop certain products that would be at the cutting edge of technology. Western corporations derided MITI because of the immense amount of free information MITI provided to Japanese companies. American companies pejoratively called all things coming from private Japanese firms as material from "Japan, Inc." Not all Japanese companies followed the directives from MITI, but this bureau influenced part of Japan's economic success.

Japan also enjoyed a sizeable literate population. Following World War II, the issue of education was prominent in all the new policies. Many believed that the reason for Japan's fall into militarism was the skewed curriculum at elementary and secondary levels. Postwar teachers instituted a more rigorous and more liberal education. At the turn of the twenty-first century, Japanese high school students rank as the world's most knowledgeable youth based on standardized testing.

Japan's growing economic leadership was evident at the 1964 Tokyo Olympics. The people and government were excited to demonstrate to the watching world that Japan had fully recovered from the horrors of World War II. Japan's image was changing from a militaristic one to that of a peaceful, prosperous, and technologically sophisticated nation. The world's fastest trains now connect Japan's four main islands.

While there are many success stories with regard to Japan's economic growth, one of the most remarkable developments in Japan's market is the growth of the auto industry. Prior to World War II, American auto executives attempted to penetrate the Japanese market, but nationalistic military leaders made sure that these foreign companies were excluded from Japan. Following World War II, the fledgling Japanese automakers were building upon their knowledge of assembling large army trucks. Toyota, a pre-World War II automaker, built a paltry three thousand vehicles a month in the mid 1940s. Many of these cars were large taxis that lumbered through Japan's narrow streets. Three things changed this weak industry and transformed it into a world leader. First, the Korean War provided Toyota an opportunity to produce a range of vehicles. Then, in the years following the Korean War, Toyota found itself in stiff competition with other Japanese companies that were moving into the auto industry. Datsun, Subaru, Honda, Mazda, Isuzu, and Mitsubishi company entrepreneurs created well-designed cars. Finally, gas prices rose in the 1970s because of the political instability in the oil-rich Middle East countries. The demand for fuel-efficient cars increased and Japanese carmakers were leaders in developing such vehicles. At the turn of the twenty-first century, the most popular cars in the United States include Honda, Nissan, and Toyota models.

Japanese–U.S. Relations

Despite being bitter enemies during World War II, Japan and the United States were the closest of allies once the fighting ceased. As time passed, however, tension arose between these countries. This friction was due to numerous factors. The United States was offended that Japan would not privately or publicly support America's efforts in Vietnam during the 1960s. Japan refused to allow U.S. warplanes to use its air space for bombing runs. Having experienced the wrath of America during an earlier war, the Japanese were not anxious for another country to undergo a similar horror.

Japan also resented America's continued occupation of Okinawa. After World War II, the Japanese were not in a position to request that the United States return this island to them. However, Okinawans wanted their island to become part of Japan once again. The United States saw the island as an unsinkable aircraft carrier in a very strategic location. It was not until 1972 that this sticking point between Japan, the United States, and the Okinawans was clarified. The Nixon administration returned Okinawa to Japan, while large U.S. military bases remain on the island.

The postwar economic alliance between Japan and the United States meant that the two countries pursued similar policies with regard to the world market. As such, American officials insisted that Japan continue to ignore the world's largest market—the People's Republic of China. After its founding in 1949, the PRC pursued Communist social and economic models. Japanese companies wanted to establish relations with the PRC, but the United States insisted that Japan refuse to recognize the existence of the world's most populous country. Japan reluctantly followed this policy of isolating China in deference to the United States. Meanwhile, the United States pursued secret diplomacy with China. The Japanese were shocked and embittered when they learned that such negotiations were taking place and that President Nixon was, in fact, going to visit China. The Japanese referred to this development as the "Nixon Shock." It was a signal to the Japanese that U.S. foreign policy was self-serving. This was further illustrated by a 1973 U.S. embargo on soybean exports. Because the Soviet Union was buying massive amounts of U.S. soybeans, the American government stopped all exportation of this product. At the time, Japan was receiving most of its soybeans, which was the foundation for protein in its diet, from the United States. While the embargo was quickly lifted, the Japanese felt betrayed once again by a country that was supposed to be their closest ally.

From the American perspective, a growing resentment against Japan's trade policies boiled over into a sentiment called "Japan bashing." American companies, particularly in the automobile industry, claimed that Japan was very willing to export its products but placed insurmountable duties and regulations on any import products. American companies laid off workers because they could not compete with Japan. Japan noted that American companies were unsuccessful in Japan because they would not learn the language and would not seek out the particular niches they could fill in foreign markets.

Japan and the Future

In 1990 the Japanese economic bubble burst. Japan was in an economic recession during the last decade of the twentieth century. Prior to this downturn, Japanese workers were guaranteed lifetime employment. A generic term for a worker was the "salary man." For several generations, job security defined Japanese employment. Professional people did not move from company to company, and one's identity was often tied to the business he or she worked for. Company loyalty was such that workers met early to exercise. Corporate officers were those who had worked their way up in a particular company. However, economic storms changed the forecast for Japanese workers and companies.

This economic bad news comes at a time when Japan is entering a period when it will need to provide government aid for an aging population. The Japanese live longer than any other group of people. By 2010 one out of every five Japanese will be over sixty-five. The younger generation will need to sustain an aging population—a responsibility that many young people find distasteful.

Of greater concern for the Japanese is what some might describe as the weightlessness of human existence. Japan's remarkable economic growth came with a heavy price. Prior to World War II Japanese were called to make sacrifices so that Japan could become a first-class nation. The nation became industrialized on the backs of the young and old. Rural farmers accepted their perpetual tenancy existence and the fact that they could not compete with landowners and cheap grain coming in from Japan's colonies. After the war, the people once again were called upon to "bear the unbearable." For several generations, Japanese workers toiled night and day to build an economic superpower. However, what one finds in Japan these days is a search for meaning in life beyond having possessions and money in the bank. There are several directions in which disillusioned Japanese are going in their search, including hedonism and religion.

Natsume Soseki (1867–1916) is often referred to as the Charles Dickens of Japan. His most famous novel, Kokoro, *explores humanity's loneliness in a modern world.*

Alcoholism among Japanese working executives is quite common. Most of these executives are men who work all day and then head to the bars. If they return home at all, they do so inebriated. Beyond drowning what they perceive as an empty existence in alcohol, however, there exists an insatiable drive for sexual pleasure in Japan. Deviant behavior in Japan has reached a point where the government is attempting to curtail certain freedoms. One somewhat disturbing example illustrates this.

As the economy began to tighten in the late 1980s, a growing number of junior high school- and high school-aged girls began engaging in prostitution. One study notes that close to one quarter of all high school Japanese girls had some connection with this practice. Termed *enjo kosai* (compensated dating), many teenage girls hook up with older men for "dates." In return for certain services, often related to sex, these young women are given money or gifts. Unlike the traditional practice of prostitution, which is often borne out of destitution, Japanese girls claim that they practice prostitution because they are bored, or wish to have extra cash to purchase the latest fashions. Many claim that they have seen their parents sacrifice everything for money. These young women can earn as much as their parents, and do so knowing that the ultimate goal of most Japanese people is economic prosperity. Of course, there must be a demand for this market to prosper. Indeed, young Japanese girls cannot satiate the number of Japanese salary men looking for dates. As such, thousands of women from throughout Asia, particularly from the Philippines, have been brought to Japan under false pretenses and eventually forced into prostitution. Travel companies offer sex tours to Japanese men, which include special trips to Thailand and the Philippines for the primary purpose of pleasure. To try to curb the growth of teenage prostitution, the Japanese government in 1997 increased the penalties for anyone who pays or otherwise compensates someone under eighteen to engage in sexual activity.

Some Japanese who are disillusioned with pure materialism turn to religion. New religions in Japan number in the thousands. Altogether, more than three thousand religions in Japan clamor for adherents. Scores of Buddhist and Shinto sects dot the religious landscape of modern Japan. While many thought that these religions were part of the fringe of Japan's society, events in the year 1995 proved that these different groups should be taken more seriously. In that year, adherents to a cult that called itself *Aum Shinrikyō* released poisonous gas in the Tokyo subway system. The material killed a dozen people and injured thousands. One of the more disturbing aspects of this event is that the members of *Aum Shinrikyō* were college-educated engineers and scientists. Their frustration with the empty life of their economically prosperous parents led to their following the orders of a cult leader.

This is the Nijubashi Bridge with the imperial palace in the background.

Conclusion

Japan's story is amazing. For the past two thousand years, the inhabitants on the small islands that make up Japan have affected the world. How is it that such an isolated group, living on inhospitable land, could have made such an impact on human history? Japan ranks as the first in many respects: it was the first Asian nation to turn back the Mongols; it was the first Asian nation to industrialize; it was the first Asian nation to cross the Pacific and attack U.S. forces; and it is the first nation to be an economic superpower while maintaining a minimal defense force. Does Japan have a secret? Why didn't other Asian nations industrialize when Japan did? How was it that Japan was able to stave off Western imperialism and, in fact, join in the colony-collecting game?

Some may answer these questions in terms of historical happenstance; others might point to providence—as the Japanese did when the *kamikaze* intervened during the Mongol invasion. To whatever one chooses to attribute Japan's successes, there are several themes in its history that point to a nation that succeeded beyond what most ever expected. These themes include Japan's willingness to learn, its martial spirit, and the Confucian social structure.

There is a false idea that Japanese are great imitators; that is, that they simply incorporate the traits and technology of more sophisticated nations. While it is true that Japan imported outside ideas, it was not a nation that simply imitated foreign patterns. In truth, Japan was happy to learn from foreigners, but it was never willing to indiscriminately adopt any alien model of religion, society, or economy. There are many illustrations of Japan choosing patterns with much prejudice. China certainly offered Japan a host of ideas and options to follow. There were elements of Chinese culture that Japan adopted, but the Japanese fit in these foreign ideas with indigenous patterns. For example, Japanese women were treated with more respect than were their Chinese sisters; promotion in Japanese politics was more often tied to nepotism than exam results; and the Japanese emperor was not seen as the mediator between heaven and earth, but as being part of heaven on earth.

When Japan was forced open in the nineteenth century by what one author calls the "predatory nature of the West," it was clear that Japan had fallen behind the emerging industrialized powers. While it is true that during the second half of the nineteenth century Japan integrated many Western ideas into its culture, from baseball to Christmas, all that was borrowed was done so discriminately. Japan's constitution is an excellent case study. As a country coming out of feudalism, Japan was aware that it needed a "modern" government to be accepted by the world's powerful nations. After signing treaties with foreign powers, the government sent a large group to travel the world and report back to the nation's officials. It was agreed that Japan had to have a constitution that was similar to that of Prussia, England, and the United States. This they did. However, the Japanese were not going to compromise their principles regarding the sovereignty of the emperor. Thus, the 1889 constitution began by noting that the emperor is sacred and inviolable. At this point, there was not a Western nation that believed that its leader was divine. But that was not going to change Japan's worldview. The Japanese were not simply going to imitate the world's greatest powers; they were going to learn from the West and fit this knowledge into a Japanese pattern. Finally, there was much that Japan learned from the United States after World War II. Nonetheless, while Japanese automakers created vehicles that appeared modest compared with the cars from America's great automakers, these automobiles were more reliable and environmentally efficient. While learning from Detroit manufacturers, the Japanese put their own twist on this industry. The results are seen in the answer to whether one would like to own a Ford Pinto or a Honda Accord.

Japan's past is dominated by a spirit of militarism. For almost one thousand years the shogun and samurai had inordinate influence in the state's political, economic, and social spheres. Power flowed from the shogun's headquarters while the samurai had such privileges that the common people did not dare look into the eyes of a member of this sword-wielding military class. Despite Japan's record of peace since World War II, one must recognize the historically dominant role of the military throughout the islands.

The militarism that shaped Japan was intimately connected to a world of discipline. A code of harsh discipline defined the military class. Indeed, the notion of self-sacrifice pervaded all society. Perhaps this helps explain Japan's meteoric rise during the Meiji era and its economic transformation after World War II.

Most states do not stay together as long as Japan has. One imperial family has remained in place for fifteen hundred years. It certainly has helped that Japan had an ethnically homogenous society and that it was somewhat geographically isolated. Nonetheless, Japanese communities were separated by bodies of water and mountainous terrain. There were many hindrances to state unity. It is, therefore, the combined elements of Confucian ethics and Buddhist doctrines that have acted as the glue that has kept Japan together through the centuries. Confucian emphasis on relationships and social harmony provided political legitimization for Japan's elite. Farmers dutifully paid their respect and taxes to the aristocrats and samurai to demonstrate their proper relationship to the higher classes. Japanese accepted their fate based on the doctrine of karma—that heaven rewards kindness and punishes evil. These paradigms remained even after the aristocrats and samurai lost their positions. For example, in today's Japan, one's identity remains intricately intertwined to the company he or she works for.

Conclusion

Twentieth-century Japanese built Asia's most formidable army and navy; they also created the planet's second-largest economy. It took sacrifice and unity to accomplish these feats. Yet, Japan's true greatness is best defined not in its martial spirit or financial institutions, but in its devotion to social harmony.

Glossary of
Japanese Names and Terms

Ainu: People from the Caucasoid race that migrated to northern Japan thousands of years ago. They were pushed north out of central Honshu by the more dominant Mongoloid peoples. Many of the Ainu settled in Japan's northern island of Hokkaido. Today about 25,000 Ainu remain, many living on government-supported reservations.

Amida: Known as the Buddha of Compassion, Amida's righteousness reportedly saves all those who place their faith in him.

Ashikaga: The weakest of the three shogunate houses that ruled Japan. The Ashikaga shoguns were in place from 1338 to 1573.

Ashikaga Takauji (1305–1358): Betrayed the Hōjō clan and subsequently ended the Kamakura *bakufu*. After siding with the independent Emperor Go-Daigo, he then turned on the emperor and established the Ashikaga shogunate (1338–1573).

Ashikaga Yoshiaki (1537–1597): The last Ashikaga shogun. He owed his position to Oda Nobunaga who subsequently turned on the Ashikaga house and ousted Yoshiaki.

Bakufu: Translated "tent government," this was the term used for the military capital of Japan as opposed to Kyoto, which was the imperial capital.

Buddhism: A religious faith founded by the Indian prince, Siddhartha Gautama (c.563–c.483 B.C.). It came to Japan by the fifth century A.D. The teachings in this faith include the assertion that all life is suffering and that the source of suffering is desire. Buddhism also emphasizes the role of karma. Humans are visited with blessings or curses based on whether they have practiced good karma or evil karma. There were various Buddhist sects that influenced Japan's society.

Chang Tso-lin (1873–1928): The Chinese warlord of Manchuria whose murder facilitated greater Japanese influence in Manchuria.

Chiang Kai-shek (1887–1975): The Chinese general who led China's Nationalist Party (Kuomintang or KMT).

Chōshū: A powerful *han* (domain) on the southwestern portion of Honshu. Chōshū was a leading *han* in the revolution that toppled the Tokugawa shogunate in 1868 and installed imperial rule in Japan.

Confucianism: A Chinese philosophy derived from the teachings of Confucius (551–479 B.C.). The ethics of this philosophy emphasize maintenance of hierarchical relationships and observance of proper protocol in all rituals.

Daimyo/Military Governors: During Tokugawa times (1600–1868), governors known as daimyo controlled more than two hundred and fifty domains. Each daimyo was charged with maintaining the peace and prosperity of his particular domain.

Edo: A small village on central Honshu's eastern shores. Edo became the capital for the Tokugawa house. By 1700 Edo was the largest city in the world. Following the end of Tokugawa rule, the emperor moved to Edo and the city's name was changed to Tokyo, or "eastern capital."

Fudai **daimyo**: Those military governors who were allied with the Tokugawa house during the East-West civil war of 1600.

Fujiwara: A powerful aristocratic family whose power increased in the ninth and tenth centuries because the imperial house chose its brides from the Fujiwara family.

Go-Daigo (1288–1339): An emperor who sought to rule in his own right following the fall of the Kamakura *bakufu*. He was betrayed by Ashikaga Takauji and he fled Kyoto. For several generations there were two competing emperors because Go-Daigo's followers supported the ousted emperor.

Han: The Japanese term for a geographical area under the control of an individual or family. In English, the term *han* is translated as "domain."

Heian: An earlier name for Kyoto. Between 780–1185, Heian was also the center of Japan's political power.

Toyotomi Hideyori (1593–1615): The only son of Toyotomi Hideyoshi. Still a boy when his father died in 1598, Hideyori and his mother moved to the Osaka castle. Despite a pledge to protect the boy and his mother, Tokugawa Ieyasu's forces attacked the Osaka castle in 1615. Hideyori and his mother died during the battle.

Toyotomi Hideyoshi (1537–1598): This common soldier's diplomatic and military skills served to unite Japan. After uniting Japan, Hideyoshi ordered the samurai to invade Korea, where the Japanese armies suffered stinging defeats.

Hirohito (1901–1989): Emperor Hirohito was Japan's longest-reigning emperor (1927–1989). Japanese historians debate the extent of Hirohito's role in propagating Japan's war against the United States.

Hōjō: The clan that raised Japan's first shogun, Minamoto Yoritomo (1147–1199). Following Yoritomo's death, Hōjō elders took the reins of power and controlled the future Kamakura shoguns from behind the scenes.

Hokkaido: Known as Ezo until the nineteenth century, this northern island was scarcely populated until after the 1868 Meiji Restoration.

Honshu: Japan's main island.

Tokugawa Ieyasu (1542–1616): The leader of Japan's eastern provinces, Ieyasu won the 1600 Battle of Sekigahara against the western military houses. In 1603 he accepted the title of shogun and his descendents ruled Japan until 1868.

Iwakura Mission: In 1871 top officials of the Meiji government went on an extensive investigatory trip to the West. Their task was to learn from the Western modern states so they could implement similar patterns in Japan.

Jimmu: The legendary first emperor of Japan. Jimmu's reign reportedly began in 660 B.C. His center of power was on the Yamato Plain and thus the imperial line, still in place today, is often referred to as the Yamato family.

Jito: The term for low-ranking samurai who served as deputies for the more powerful military leaders.

Jōmon: The earliest civilization in Japan, whose end in 250 B.C. paved the way for the Yayoi civilization. Jōmon culture is distinguished by the type of pottery decorations found from this period. These embellishments included patterns of rope pressed into the pottery.

Kamakura: A geographical location east of Kyoto where the first *bakufu* was located. From 1185 to 1333, also known as the Kamakura era, the locus of power was at the *bakufu*.

Kuomintang (KMT): The Chinese Nationalist Party founded by Dr. Sun Yat-sen (1866–1925). The Japanese army was unable to defeat the KMT despite an eight-year (1937–1945) occupation of China.

Kami: A Shinto term meaning a god.

Kamikaze "The Divine Wind": A god in the Shinto pantheon (or an embodiment of divine providence) credited for destroying the thirteenth-century Mongol invading force.

Kublai Khan (1215–1294): The grandson of the great unifier of Mongol tribes, Ghengis Khan, Kublai Khan conquered China and Korea but was unsuccessful in his multiple attempts to conquer Japan.

Kwantung Army: The portion of Japan's army that fought the Russians in Manchuria during 1905. The Kwantung Army remained in Manchuria and its aggressive, autonomous actions eventually led to Japan's invasion of China in 1937.

Kyoto: The imperial capital of China from the ninth century to 1868. It was also the center for many Buddhist sects and Japan's silk industry.

Kyushu: The southernmost of Japan's largest islands. Most early migration into Japan and later international trade took place in Kyushu.

Legalism: A Chinese philosophy that opposed the Confucian idea of the innate goodness of human nature. Legalists believed that society was kept in line by strict rules, harsh punishments, and extravagant rewards.

Manchukuo: A puppet state that Japan created in 1932. Manchukuo was formerly known as Manchuria, an area of northeast China. Japan's creation of Manchukuo was condemned by the League of Nations, which prompted Japan's withdrawal from that body.

Manchuria: The northeast portion of China where Japanese and Russian troops fought during the 1904–1905 Russo-Japanese War. After the war Japan kept its army in Manchuria. In 1932 Manchuria declared itself an independent state (though it was controlled by Japan), called Manchukuo

Meiji: The reign name given to Emperor Mutsuhito (r. 1868–1912).

Meiji Constitution: On January 1, 1889, the Meiji Emperor gave a new constitution to Japan. Architects of this constitution wanted the document to mirror the constitutions of modern Western states. This began representative government in Japan, with two houses that made up the diet. However, this document was unique from Western constitutions in that the Meiji constitution began with the assertion that the emperor was sacred and inviolable.

Minamoto: A powerful military clan that sided with the Fujiwara house in the twelfth-century civil war.

Minamoto Yoritomo (1147–1199): The first shogun to move the center of power from Kyoto to the *bakufu*.

Muromachi: A geographical area outside of Kyoto from which the Ashikaga shoguns ruled. The Muromachi period (1338–1573) was an era when both the imperial and shogun houses were financially and politically weak.

Nagasaki: A port town on the west coast of Kyushu. Nagasaki was the center of international trade during the Tokugawa era (1600–1868).

Nara: From 710 to 794 the imperial family lived on this plain, just south of Kyoto.

Oda Nobunaga (1534–1582): After a century of incessant civil war, Oda Nobunaga began the process of state unification. He was assassinated before Japan was fully unified, but one of his generals, Toyotomi Hideyoshi (1536–1598), completed the process.

Ōjin (346–395): In the Japanese historical chronicles, Ōjin is reportedly the fifteenth of the Yamato emperors. It is possible that he, in fact, was the founder of the Yamato dynasty.

Okinawa: The largest island in the Ryukyu Island Chain, south of Kyushu. During the last months of World War II, there was a fierce battle for the control of Okinawa. After World War II, American forces continued to control Okinawa until May 15, 1972, when the administration of Okinawa reverted to the Japanese government.

Osaka: During the Tokugawa era (1600–1868) Osaka was one of the three big cities; the other two were Edo and Kyoto. Osaka's geographical proximity to the edge of Japan's Inland Sea made it a convenient location for merchants transferring material from east and west. Osaka became the central rice market for Japan, with warehouses dotting the city's landscape. By 1700 there were thirteen hundred rice brokers in Osaka.

Paekche: A Korean state that reportedly introduced Buddhism to Japan in the fifth century A.D.

Takamori Saigō (1827–1877): A Satsuma leader who was a key advisor in the early Meiji era. Disgruntled with the policies toward the samurai, Saigō was a leader in a rebellion against the government. He died during this 1877 rebellion.

Samurai: Japan's military class. In the hierarchy of social classes, the samurai were at the top with exclusive rights to owning a surname and wearing a sword.

Sankin kotai: During the Tokugawa era (1600–1868), military governors were required to live in the shogun's capital of Edo every other year. This practice was termed *sankin kotai* or alternate attendance.

Sekigahara: An area in central Honshu where the eastern armies led by Tokugawa Ieyasu defeated the western generals in 1600. Tokugawa's victory established him as the country's new military leader.

Seventeen-Article Constitution: In 604 Prince Shōtoku reportedly produced Japan's first enduring political document. Consisting of seventeen points, this essay is known as the Seventeen-Article Constitution. Its primary significance is that it demonstrated the court's desire to incorporate Chinese philosophy and religion into the Japanese political and social systems.

Shintoism: A religion indigenous to Japan. This faith emphasizes the simplicity of worship, physical purity, and reverence for things that inspire a sense of awe.

Shoen: Tax-free land given to individuals by the emperor. Initially, these imperial land grants were miniscule in size. However, *shoen* proprietors clandestinely increased these tax-free zones and by the twelfth century one-half of Japan's lands consisted of these estates.

Shogun: An abbreviation for *seii taishogun* or "barbarian-suppressing general." This title was bestowed by the emperor to the leading military general whose blood lines were traced to the Minamoto family.

Prince Shōtoku: A leader of the Soga clan, Shōtoku was appointed as a regent to the empress in 593. As a devout Buddhist, Shōtoku worked for the next thirty years to incorporate this faith into the imperial household. Shōtoku might represent a movement toward Buddhism and Chinese influence more than just one individual.

Shōwa: The title of the era when Emperor Hirohito reigned (1926–1989). An English translation for the word Shōwa is "Bright Peace."

Shugo: Military sheriffs who were called on to keep order in specific geographical areas. They were assisted in this duty by their deputies, also known as *jito*.

Soga clan: An aristocratic family whose influence led to the acceptance of Buddhism at the imperial court during the sixth and seventh centuries.

Taira house: A leading military family that sided with the imperial house during the twelfth-century civil war.

Taishō: The title of the era when Emperor Yoshihito reigned over Japan (1912–1926). An English translation of the word Taishō is "Great Righteousness."

T'ang China: A Chinese dynasty that lasted from 618–907. Also known as China's golden age, T'ang China heavily influenced the social and political structures of Japan.

Tokyo: See Edo.

Tozama **daimyo**: Military governors who were not allies with the Tokugawa house during the 1600 Battle of Sekigahara. Nonetheless, Tokugawa Ieyasu incorporated *tozama* daimyo into his system of daimyo/*bakufu* rule.

Uji: The Japanese term for clan. The earliest social organizations in Japan revolved around the different clans throughout the islands.

Versailles: A small town outside of Paris where the World War I victors gathered in 1919 to map out a peace treaty. At Versailles, Japan was considered one of the top five powers in the world.

Yamato: A plain on the western portion of Honshu, Japan's largest island. The legendary first emperors of Japan were said to have ruled from the Yamato Plain. Yamato also refers to an era in Japan that lasted from A.D. 250–710.

Yayoi: The title of an era in Japan (250 B.C.–A.D. 250). Yayoi civilization was agriculturally more sophisticated than Jōmon society (2500–250 B.C.). The term Yayoi is derived from a geographical area on the periphery of Tokyo where, in 1948, artifacts of Yayoi culture were found.

Yoshida Shigeru (1878–1967): The Japanese politician who worked with the post-World War II occupying force. He was famous for saying that while Japan lost the war, it could win the peace.

Zaibatsu: Large companies where all aspects of production were monopolized by the corporation. A *zaibatsu* often was led by one extended family.

Zen Buddhism: A form of Buddhism that emphasizes mental and physical discipline along with meditation.

Bibliography

Beasley, W.G. *The Japanese Experience: A Short History of Japan*. Los Angeles: University of California Press, 1999.

———. *The Meiji Restoration*. Stanford, California: Stanford University Press, 1972.

Bellah, Robert N. *Tokugawa Religion: The Values of Pre-Industrial Japan*. New York: Collier-Macmillan, 1957.

Berry, Mary Elizabeth. *The Culture of Civil War in Kyoto*. Los Angeles: University of California Press, 1994.

———. *Hideyoshi*. Cambridge, Massachusetts: Harvard University Press, 1982.

Bix, Herbert P. *Hirohito and the Making of Modern Japan*. New York: HarperCollins Publishers, 2000.

Cooper, Michael, Editor. *They Came to Japan: An Anthology of European Reports on Japan, 1543–1640*. London: Thames & Hudson, 1965.

Craig, Albert M. *The Heritage of Japanese Civilization*. Upper Saddle River, New Jersey: Prentice Hall, 2003.

Dower, John W. *Embracing Defeat: Japan in the Wake of World War II*. New York: W.W. Norton & Company, 1999.

Elison, George. *Deus Destroyed: The Image of Christianity in Early Modern Japan*. Cambridge, Massachusetts: Harvard University Press, 1973.

Gluck, Carol. *Japan's Modern Myths: Ideology in the Late Meiji Period*. Princeton, New Jersey: Princeton University Press, 1985.

Hall, John Whitney. *Early Modern Japan*. The Cambridge History of Japan, vol. 4. New York: Cambridge University Press, 1991.

———, Nagahara Keiji, and Kozo Yamamura, Editors. *Japan Before Tokugawa: Political Consolidation and Economic Growth 1500–1650*. Princeton, New Jersey: Princeton University Press, 1981.

———, and Marius B. Jansen, Editors. *Studies in the Institutional History of Early Modern Japan*. Princeton, New Jersey: Princeton University Press, 1968.

Hanley, Susan B. *Everyday Things in Pre-Modern Japan: The Hidden Legacy of Material Culture*. Los Angeles: University of California Press, 1997.

Henshall, Kenneth G. *A History of Japan: From Stone Age to Superpower*. New York: St. Martin's Press, 1999.

Ishizawa, Masao et. al. *The Heritage of Japanese Art*. New York: Kodansha International, 1982.

Jansen, Marius B. *The Making of Modern Japan*. Cambridge, Massachusetts: Belknap, 2000.

———, Editor. *The Nineteenth Century*. The Cambridge History of Japan, vol. 5. New York: Cambridge University Press, 1989.

Keene, Donald. *The Japanese Discovery of Europe, 1720–1830*. Revised. Stanford, California: Stanford University Press, 1969.

Lehmann, Jean-Pierre. *The Roots of Modern Japan*. New York: St. Martin's Press, 1982.

Leupp, Gary P. *Male Colors: The Construction of Homosexuality in Tokugawa Japan*. Los Angeles: University of California Press, 1995.

———. *Servants, Shophands, and Laborers in the Cities of Tokugawa Japan*. Princeton, New Jersey: Princeton University Press, 1992.

Lu, David J., Editor. *Japan: A Documentary History* Volume 1, The Dawn of History to the Late Tokugawa Period. New York: M. E. Sharpe, 1997.

———, Editor. *Japan: A Documentary History* Volume 2, The Late Tokugawa Period to the Present. New York: M. E. Sharpe, 1997.

Maruyama, Masao. *Studies in the Intellectual History of Tokugawa Japan*. Translated by Mikiso Hane. Princeton, New Jersey: Princeton University Press, 1974.

Mason, Penelope. *History of Japanese Art*. New York: Harry N. Abrams, Inc., Publishers, 1993.

Matsunosuke, Nishiyama. *Edo Culture: Daily Life and Diversions in Urban Japan, 1600–1868*. Translated by Gerald Groemer. Honolulu: University of Hawaii Press, 1997.

McClain, James L. *A Modern History of Japan*. New York: W.W. Norton & Company, 2002.

Nakane, Chie and Shinzaburo Oishi, Editors. *Tokugawa Japan: The Social and Economic Antecedents of Modern Japan*. Translated by Conrad Totman. Tokyo: University of Tokyo Press, 1990.

Ooms, Herman. *Tokugawa Ideology: Early Constructs, 1570–1680*. Princeton, New Jersey: Princeton University Press, 1985.

Plummer, Katherine. *The Shogun's Reluctant Ambassadors: Japanese Sea Drifters in the North Pacific*. North Pacific Studies Series, vol. 17. Portland, Oregon: Oregon Historical Society, 1991.

Sansom, George. *A History of Japan 1615–1867*. Stanford: Stanford University Press, 1963.

Seiroku, Noma. *The Arts of Japan: Ancient and Medieval*. Translated by John Rosenfield. Tokyo: Kodansha International, 1966.

Shiba, Ryotaro. *The Last Shogun: The Life of Tokugawa Yoshinobu*. Translated by Juliet Winters Carpenter. Tokyo: Kodansha International, 1998.

Smith, Bradley. *Japan: A History in Art*. Garden City, New York: Doubleday & Company, Inc., 1964.

Smith, Thomas C. *The Agrarian Origins of Modern Japan*. Stanford, California: Stanford University Press, 1959.

———. *Native Sources of Japanese Industrialization, 1750–1920*. Los Angeles: University of California Press, 1988.

Smith, Thomas C., Robert Y. Eng, and Robert T. Lundy. *Nakahara: Family Farming and Population in a Japanese Village, 1717–1830*. Stanford, California: Stanford University Press, 1977.

Smitka, Michael, Editor. *The Japanese Economy in the Tokugawa Era, 1600–1868*. New York: Garland Publishing, Inc., 1998.

Totman, Conrad. *Tokugawa Ieyasu: Shogun*. Union City, California: Heian International Inc., 1983.

Vlastos, Stephen. *Peasant Protests and Uprisings in Tokugawa Japan*. Los Angeles: University of California Press, 1986.

Walthall, Anne, Editor. *Peasant Uprisings in Japan*. Chicago: University of Chicago Press, 1991.

Webb, Herschel. *The Japanese Imperial Institution in the Tokugawa Period*. New York: Columbia University Press, 1968.

Yoshikawa, Eiji. *Musashi*. Translated by Charles S. Terry. New York: Harper & Row Publishers, 1971.

Index

Index